Lucian's
Dialogues
of the Sea Gods

An Intermediate Greek Reader

Greek text with running vocabulary and commentary

Stephanie Krause
Evan Hayes
Stephen Nimis

Lucian's *Dialogues of the Sea Gods*: An Intermediate Greek Reader: Greek text with running vocabulary and commentary

First Edition

© 2014 by Evan Hayes and Stephen Nimis

All rights reserved. Subject to the exception immediately following, this book may not be reproduced, in whole or in part, in any form (beyond copying permitted by Sections 107 and 108 of the U.S. Copyright Law and except by reviewers for the public press), without written permission from the publisher. The authors have made a version of this work available (via email) under a Creative Commons Attribution-Noncommercial-Share Alike 3.0 License. The terms of the license can be accessed at www.creativecommons.org.

Accordingly, you are free to copy, alter and distribute this work under the following conditions:

    1. You must attribute the work to the author (but not in a way that suggests that the author endorses your alterations to the work).

    2. You may not use this work for commercial purposes.

    3. If you alter, transform or build up this work, you may distribute the resulting work only under the same or similar license as this one.

ISBN-10: 1940997089

ISBN-13: 978-1940997087

Published by Faenum Publishing, Ltd.

Cover Design: Evan Hayes

Fonts: Garamond
            GFS Porson

editor@faenumpublishing.com

Table of Contents

Acknowledgements v

Introduction ix

Abbreviations xiii

Text and Commentary 1-76

Grammatical Topics
    Present General Conditions 6
    Translating Participles 8
    Potential Optatives 9
    Imperatives 10
    Participles: General Principles 12
    οἶδα and εἶδον 23
    Other General or Indefinite Clauses 24
    The Different Meanings of αὐτός 25
    Result Clauses 26
    Circumstantial Participles 29
    More Conditions 31
    αὐτός again 42

List of Verbs 78-87

Glossary 89-94

Acknowledgments

The idea for this project grew out of work that we, the authors, did with support from Miami University's Undergraduate Summer Scholars Program, for which we thank Martha Weber and the Office of Advanced Research and Scholarship. The Miami University College of Arts and Science's Dean's Scholar Program allowed us to continue work on the project and for this we are grateful to the Office of the Dean, particularly to Phyllis Callahan and Nancy Arthur for their continued interest and words of encouragement.

Work on the series, of which this volume is a part, was generously funded by the Joanna Jackson Goldman Memorial Prize through the Honors Program at Miami University. We owe a great deal to Carolyn Haynes, and the 2010 Honors & Scholars Program Advisory Committee for their interest and confidence in the project.

The technical aspects of the project were made possible through the invaluable advice and support of Bill Hayes, Christopher Kuo, and Daniel Meyers. The equipment and staff of Miami University's Interactive Language Resource Center were a great help along the way. We are also indebted to the Perseus Project, especially Gregory Crane and Bridget Almas, for their technical help and resources.

Special thanks to Mark Lightman, whose enthusiasm for these volumes early on, and especially for the works of Lucian, has inspired us to keep moving forward.

We also profited greatly from advice and help on the POD process from Geoffrey Steadman. All responsibility for errors, however, rests with the authors themselves.

caris parentibus
Dana and Ronald Krause

Introduction

The aim of this book is to make Lucian's *Dialogues of the Sea Gods* accessible to intermediate students of Ancient Greek. The running vocabulary and grammatical commentary are meant to provide everything necessary to read each page so that readers can progress through the text, improving their knowledge of Greek while enjoying one of the most entertaining authors of antiquity.

Lucian's *Dialogues of the Sea Gods* is a great text for intermediate readers. The dialogues are breezy and fun to read with relatively simple sentence structure. Typical for Lucian, classical literature is the source for most of the material, with amusing takes on traditional stories and scenarios. Sea deities tend to be rather minor characters in Greek myths, and in these texts we see Lucian recasting some famous incidents by centralizing the point of view of such minor characters: Nereids, dolphins, fountains, winds, and even the Sea herself weigh in on various events and present novel narrative perspectives on them.

For instance, the second dialogue picks up on an episode in book 9 of the *Odyssey*, when Polyphemus prays to Poseidon to punish Odysseus for his blinding. Lucian expands on the Cyclops' request by adding the reaction of Poseidon to the incident. In this exchange, it is clear that Poseidon has sympathy for his son, but he also reveals that he knows Polyphemus is not too sharp. This expansion of a popular Homeric episode introduces a comedic element that is not explicit in the epic, but is just below the surface. Since the episode in the *Odyssey* is recounted by Odysseus himself, Lucian provides us with the "rest of the story," so to speak, by giving us the Cyclops' own account.

Dialogue four expands another episode in the *Odyssey*, this time about Menelaus' detention in Egypt on his way back from the war. Homer has the Spartan king relate his encounter with Proteus, who has the power to change himself into anything he wishes. In Lucian's dialogue, Menelaus can accept the fact that Proteus can change himself into water, but is astonished that he is able to become fire; he suspects that Proteus is deceiving him and that it is all an optical illusion. Proteus offers Menelaus the opportunity to touch him when he changes into fire, but Menelaus demurs. Here Lucian plays on one of his favorite themes, the improbabilities and absurdities of canonical stories.

Lucian

These two dialogues exemplify well the parodic character of Lucian's divine dialogues, as explained by B. Branham: "By reproducing the model's features selectively, they emphasize the artifice of the original version in the distorted image of the parody .... Lucian will make the subject comic through tonal devices and strategic omissions--exaggeration, ellipsis, misplaced emphasis--that accentuate the indigenous peculiarities of a familiar world" (Branham 1989, 134). In each dialogue, the situation will be a familiar one, but Lucian will fasten on some minor element to cast a new light on it.

The inspiration of Hellensitic literature is most clear in the first dialogue, whose theme, the love of Galatea and Polyphemus, is treated twice by Theocritus (3rd century BCE). The *Europa* of Moschus (fl. 150 BCE) is a possible inspiration for dialogue 15, and also has a description of Io's flight to Egypt, which may have inspired dialogue 7. But the more general Hellenistic interest in minor characters and unusual myths is also shared by Lucian in these short and witty pieces. It has also been suggested that the visual arts may have been an inspiration for some of these dialogues, which puts them in contact with another preoccupation of imperial literature, descriptions of works of art. Lucian himself produced a number of rhetorical descriptions, especially in *On his House*, so this is a reasonable assumption. Bartley notes that the following scenarios were famous in the visual arts: the abduction of Europa (15), the blinding of the Cyclops (2), the judgment of Paris (5), the rescue of Arion (8), and the rescue of Andromeda (14).

There is also some interplay among the dialogues themselves. For example, parts of the story of Perseus are told in dialogues 12 and 14; dialogues 8 and 9 both mention the fate of Ino and her children, although in the former she is not the main theme. The winds Zephyrus and Notus appear in 7 and 15 discussing amorous adventures of Zeus. As the most important sea god, Poseidon is an interlocutor in seven of the dialogues.

Two excellent literary commentaries have been published on the *Dialogues of the Sea Gods* recently: A. N. Bartley, *Lucian's Dialogi Marini* (Newcastle: Cambridge Scholars, 2009) and Keith Sidwell, *Lucian : selections edited with notes and vocabulary* (Bristol, England : Bristol Classical Press, 1986). These texts contain interpretive essays and detailed information about sources, which is summarized briefly in the introduction to each dialogue below. The idiomatic translation by H. W. and H. G. Fowler can be found online at http://www.theoi.com (not including the marginally scandalous dialogue of Enipeus and Poseidon). M. D. Macleod's Loeb version with Greek and English on facing pages, is also available online in pdf format.

The Greek text is that of K. Jacobitz (1896), which has been digitized by the Perseus Project and made available with a Creative Commons license, as is our text. Here and there we have made minor changes to the text in the name of readability. This is not a scholarly edition; for that one should turn to the OCT of Macleod.

There are two numbering systems for the dialogues reflecting two manuscript traditions. The numbers used here are from the edition of Jacobitz. Where they differ from the other numbering system, found in the Loeb and elsewhere, we have put the alternate number in parentheses.

Select Bibliography

Bartley, Adam. "Techniques of Composition in Lucian's Minor Dialogues." *Hermes* 133.3 (2005), 358-367.

Bompaire, J. *Lucien Écrivain: Imitation et Création*. Paris, 1958.

Branham, R. Bracht. *Unruly Eloquence: Lucian and the Comedy of Traditions*. Harvard University Press: Cambridge, 1987.

Deferrari, R. J. *Lucian's Atticism*. Hackert :Amsterdam, 1969.

Householder, F. W. *Literary Quotation and Allusion in Lucian*. King's Crown Press: Morningside Heights, 1941.

How to use this book

The page-by-page vocabularies gloss all but the most common words. We have endeavored to make these glossaries as useful as possible without becoming fulsome. All words occurring frequently in the text can be found in an appendix in the back, but it is our hope that most readers will not need to use this appendix often.

The commentary is almost exclusively grammatical, explaining subordinate clauses, unusual verb forms, and idioms. Brief summaries of a number of grammatical and morphological topics are interspersed through the text as well, and there is a list of verbs used by Lucian that have unusual forms in an appendix. The principal parts of those verbs are given there rather than in the glossaries. A good reading strategy is to read a passage in Greek, check the glossary for unusual words and consult the commentary as a last resort.

An Important Disclaimer:

This volume is a self-published "Print on Demand" (POD) book, and it has not been vetted or edited in the usual way by publishing professionals. There are sure to be some factual and typographical errors in the text, for which we apologize in advance. The volume is also available only through online distributors, since each book is printed when ordered online. However, this publishing channel and format also account for the low price of the book; and it is a simple matter to make changes when they come to our attention. For this reason, any corrections or suggestions for improvement are welcome and will be addressed as quickly as possible in future versions of the text.

Please e-mail corrections or suggestions to editor@faenumpublishing.com.

About the Authors:

Stephanie Krause is a recent graduate in Classics at Miami University.

Evan Hayes is a recent graduate in Classics and Philosophy at Miami University and the 2011 Joanna Jackson Goldman Scholar.

Stephen Nimis is an Emeritus Professor of Classics at Miami University and Professor of English and Comparative Literature at the American University in Cairo.

Abbreviations

abs.	absolute	n.	neuter
acc.	accusative	nom.	nominative
act.	active	obj.	object
adj.	adjective	opt.	optative
adv.	adverb, adverbial	part.	participle
aor.	aorist	pass.	passive
art.	article	perf.	perfect
cl.	clause	pl.	plural
compl.	complementary	plupf.	pluperfect
cond.	condition	pot.	potential
dat.	dative	pr.	present
dir.	direct	pred.	predicate
epex.	epexegetic	pron.	pronoun
f.	feminine	purp.	purpose
fut.	future	quest.	question
gen.	genitive, general	rel.	relative
imper.	imperative	res.	result
impers.	impersonal	resp.	respect
impf.	imperfect	s.	singular
ind.	indicative	sec.	secondary
inf.	infinitive	seq.	sequence
instr.	instrumental	st.	statement
m.	masculine	subj.	subject, subjunctive
mid.	middle	temp.	temporal

ΛΟΥΚΙΑΝΟΥ
ἘΝΑΛΙΟΙ ΔΙΑΛΟΓΟΙ

Lucian's
Dialogues of the Sea Gods

1. Doris and Galatea

The subject of this dialogue, the romance between the Cyclops Polyphemus and the Nereid Galatea, is mentioned in several sources. Theocritus treats the theme twice in very different ways. In Idyll 6, Galatea is flirting with Polyphemus, who is playing hard to get. In Idyll 11, Polyphemus is distraught over the unrequited love of the nymph and consoles himself by writing poetry. Lucian gives an unusual twist to this material by having Galatea boast of the Cyclops' attentions, while her sister, Doris, insists that such a love is nothing to brag about.

ΔΩΡΙΣ: Καλὸν ἐραστήν, ὦ Γαλάτεια, τὸν Σικελὸν τοῦτον ποιμένα φασὶν ἐπιμεμηνέναι σοί.

ΓΑΛΑΤΕΙΑ: Μὴ σκῶπτε, Δωρί· Ποσειδῶνος γὰρ υἱός ἐστιν, ὁποῖος ἂν ᾖ.

ΔΩΡΙΣ: Τί οὖν; εἰ καὶ τοῦ Διὸς αὐτοῦ παῖς ὢν ἄγριος οὕτως καὶ λάσιος ἐφαίνετο καί, τὸ πάντων ἀμορφότατον, μονόφθαλμος, οἴει τὸ γένος ἄν τι ὀνῆσαι αὐτὸν πρὸς τὴν μορφήν;

ἄγριος, -α, -ον: savage
ἄμορφος, -ον: misshapen, unsightly
Γαλάτεια, ἡ: Galatea
γένος, -ους, τό: a race, stock, family
Δωρίς, -δος, ἡ: Doris
ἐπιμαίνομαι: to be mad
ἐραστής, -οῦ, ὁ: a lover
Ζεύς, Διός, ὁ: Zeus
καλός, -η, -ον: handsome
λάσιος, -ον: hairy, rough, shaggy, woolly
μονόφθαλμος, -ον: one-eyed
μορφή, ἡ: a form, shape

οἶμαι: to suppose, think
ὀνίνημι: to profit, benefit, help, assist
ὁποῖος: of what sort or quality
παῖς, παιδός, ὁ: a child
ποιμήν, -ένος, ὁ: a herdsman
Ποσειδῶν, -ῶνος, ὁ: Poseidon
Σικελός, -ή, -όν: Sicilian, of or from Sicily
σκώπτω: to hoot, mock, jeer, scoff at
υἱός, ὁ: a son
φαίνομαι: to appear
φημί: to declare, make known

ἐπιμεμηνέναι: perf. inf. in ind. st. after φασιν, "they say that this herdsman *has become mad*"
σοί: dat. of advantage after ἐπιμεμηνέναι, "mad *for you*"
μὴ σκῶπτε: pr. imper., "do not mock!"
ὁποῖος ἂν ᾖ: pr. subj. in general rel. cl., "whatever sort he is"
εἰ καὶ … ὤν: pr. part. representing impf. tense in pr. contrafactual protasis, "*even if he were* Zeus's son"
ἐφαίνετο: impf. also a contrafactual protasis, "*if he continued to appear* so savage"
ἄν τι ὀνῆσαι: aor. inf. of ὀνίνημι in ind. st. after οἴει, representing an aor. indic. in a past contrafactual apodosis, "do you suppose that his birth *would have benefited at all*"

ΓΑΛΑΤΕΙΑ: Οὐδὲ τὸ λάσιον αὐτοῦ καί, ὡς φής, ἄγριον ἄμορφόν ἐστιν — ἀνδρῶδες γάρ — ὅ τε ὀφθαλμὸς ἐπιπρέπει τῷ μετώπῳ οὐδὲν ἐνδεέστερον ὁρῶν ἢ εἰ δὔ ἦσαν.

ΔΩΡΙΣ: Ἔοικας, ὦ Γαλάτεια, οὐκ ἐραστὴν ἀλλ᾽ ἐρώμενον ἔχειν τὸν Πολύφημον, οἷα ἐπαινεῖς αὐτόν.

ΓΑΛΑΤΕΙΑ: Οὐκ ἐρώμενον, ἀλλὰ τὸ πάνυ ὀνειδιστικὸν τοῦτο οὐ φέρω ὑμῶν, καί μοι δοκεῖτε ὑπὸ φθόνου αὐτὸ ποιεῖν, ὅτι ποιμαίνων ποτὲ ἀπὸ τῆς σκοπῆς παιζούσας ἡμᾶς ἰδὼν ἐπὶ τῆς ᾐόνος ἐν τοῖς πρόποσι τῆς Αἴτνης,

---

ἄγριος, -α, -ον: savage
Αἴτνη, ἡ: Mt. Aetna, in Sicily
ἄμορφος, -ον: misshapen, unsightly
ἀνδρώδης, -ες: manly
δοκέω: to seem to (+ *inf.*)
ἐνδεής, -ές: deficient
ἔοικα: to seem to (+ *inf.*)
ἐπαινέω: to approve, applaud, commend
ἐπιπρέπω: to be suitable to (+ *dat.*)
ἐραστής, -οῦ, ὁ: a lover
ἐράω: to love
ᾐών, ᾐόνος, ἡ: beach, shore

λάσιος, -ον: hairy, rough, shaggy, woolly
μέτωπον, τό: a brow, forehead
ὀνειδιστικός, -ή, -όν: reproachful, abusive
ὁράω: to see
ὀφθαλμός, ὁ: an eye
παίζω: to play like a child, to sport, play
ποιμαίνω: to be shepherd
πρόπους, -ποδος, ὁ: the projecting foot of a mountain, its lowest part
σκοπή, ἡ: a lookout-place, watchtower
φέρω: to bear
φθόνος, ὁ: ill-will, envy, jealousy

τὸ λάσιον: the article makes the adj. a noun, "his shagginess"
ἐνδεέστερον: acc. n. s. adverbial, "seeing *more deficiently* not at all"
ἢ εἰ δὔ ἦσαν: expressing comparison after ἐνδεέστερον, "than if there were two"
ἐραστὴν: acc. pred., "to have Polyphemus not *as a lover*"
ἐρώμενον: pr. pass. part. of ἐράω, "but as *a beloved*"
οἷα: acc. pl. n. of respect, "*because of the sort of things* you praise him for"
τὸ πάνυ ὀνειδιστικὸν: the article makes the adj., with its adverb, a noun phrase, "the excessive abuse"
ὑπὸ φθόνου: "motivated *by ill-will*," using the agency expression
ὅτι ... προσέβλεψεν: aor. of προς-βλέπω, "because he looked at"
παιζούσας: pr. part. acc. pl. f. agreeing with ἡμᾶς, "having seen us *playing*"
ἰδὼν: aor. part. of ὁράω, "having seen"

καθ' ὃ μεταξὺ τοῦ ὄρους καὶ τῆς θαλάττης αἰγιαλὸς ἀπομηκύνεται, ὑμᾶς μὲν οὐδὲ προσέβλεψεν ἐγὼ δὲ ἐξ ἁπασῶν ἡ καλλίστη ἔδοξα, καὶ μόνη ἐμοὶ ἐπεῖχε τὸν ὀφθαλμόν. ταῦτα ὑμᾶς ἀνιᾷ· δεῖγμα γάρ, ὡς ἀμείνων εἰμὶ καὶ ἀξιέραστος, ὑμεῖς δὲ παρώφθητε.

ΔΩΡΙΣ: Εἰ ποιμένι καὶ ἐνδεεῖ τὴν ὄψιν καλὴ ἔδοξας, ἐπίφθονος οἴει γεγονέναι; καίτοι τί ἄλλο ἐν σοὶ ἐπαινέσαι εἶχεν ἢ τὸ λευκὸν μόνον; καὶ τοῦτο, οἶμαι, ὅτι συνήθης ἐστὶ τυρῷ καὶ γάλακτι· πάντα οὖν τὰ ὅμοια τούτοις ἡγεῖται

αἰγιαλός, ὁ: a shore, beach, strand
ἀμείνων, -ον: better
ἀνιάω: to grieve, distress
ἀξιέραστος, -ον: worthy of love
ἅπας, ἅπασα, ἅπαν: all, every, whole
ἀπομηκύνω: to prolong, draw out
γάλα, -ακτος, τό: milk
δεῖγμα, -ατος, τό: proof
δοκέω: to seem to be to (+ dat.)
ἐνδεής, -ές: deficient, lacking
ἐπέχω: to fix X (acc.) upon Y (dat.)
ἐπίφθονος, -ον: enviable
ἔχω: to be able to (+ inf.)
ἡγέομαι: to consider

θάλαττα, ἡ: the sea
καίτοι: and yet
λευκός, -ή, -όν: light, white, brilliant
μεταξύ: between (+ gen.)
μόνος, -η, -ον: alone, only
οἶμαι: to suppose, think
ὅμοιος, -α, -ον: like, resembling (+ dat.)
ὄρος, -ους, τό: a mountain, hill
ὄψις, ἡ: a look, appearance, aspect
παροράω: to overlook, neglect
ποιμήν, -ένος, ὁ: a herdsman
προσβλέπω: to look at
συνήθης, -ες: habituated, accustomed to (+ dat.)
τυρός, ὁ: cheese

καθ' ὅ (=κατὰ ὅ): rel. pron., "at the very point where"
ὑμᾶς μὲν ... ἐγὼ δὲ: "*while you* he did not look at ... *but I* seemed"
ἡ καλλίστη: nom. pred., "I seemed *the most beautiful one*"
ἐπεῖχε: impf. of ἐπι-έχω, "he was fixing upon" + dat.
παρώφθητε: aor. pass. from παρά-οράω, "you have been neglected."
τὴν ὄψιν: acc. of respect with ἐνδεεῖ, "lacking *in respect to his sight*"
καλὴ: nom. pred., "if you seemed to be *beautiful*"
γεγονέναι: perf. inf. of γίγνομαι in ind. st. after οἴει, "do you suppose *that you have become*"
τί ἄλλο ... ἢ, "what other thing ... than"
εἶχεν: impf., "was he able to?" + inf.
τὸ λευκὸν: "your whiteness"

καλά. ἐπεὶ τά γε ἄλλα ὁπόταν ἐθελήσῃς μαθεῖν, οἷα τυγχάνεις οὖσα τὴν ὄψιν, ἀπὸ πέτρας τινός, εἴ ποτε γαλήνη εἴη, ἐπικύψασα ἐς τὸ ὕδωρ ἰδὲ σεαυτὴν οὐδὲν ἄλλο ἢ χροίαν λευκὴν ἀκριβῶς: οὐκ ἐπαινεῖται δὲ τοῦτο, ἢν μὴ ἐπιπρέπῃ αὐτῷ καὶ τὸ ἐρύθημα.

ἀκριβής, -ές: exact, precise
γαλήνη, ἡ: a stillness of the sea, calm
ἐθέλω: to will, wish, purpose
ἐπαινέω: to approve, applaud, commend
ἐπικύπτω: to bend oneself or stoop over
ἐπιπρέπω: to be visible in addition to (+ dat.)
ἐρύθημα, -ατος, τό: a redness on the skin
λευκός, -ή, -όν: light, bright, brilliant

μανθάνω: to learn
οἷος, -α, ον: what sort of
ὁπόταν: whensoever (+ *subj.*)
ὄψις, ἡ: a look, appearance, aspect
πέτρα, ἡ: a rock, a ledge or shelf of rock
τυγχάνω: to happen to (+ *part.*)
ὕδωρ, -ατος, τό: water
χροιά, ἡ: skin

καλά: neut. acc. pred., "he considers to be *beautiful*"

τά ἄλλα: acc. of respect, "concerning other beauties"

ὁπόταν ἐθελήσῃς: aor. subj. in gen. temp. cl., "whenever you wish" + inf.

τὴν ὄψιν: acc. of respect, "to be *in appearance*"

εἴ ποτε εἴη: pr. opt. in pr. gen. protasis (where the subj. would be usual), "if ever there is calm"

ἐπικύψασα: aor. part., "having stooped over"

ἰδὲ: aor. imper. of **ὁράω**, "*just see* yourself"

οὐδὲν ἄλλο ἢ: pred. acc. with σεαυτήν, "yourself to be *nothing other than*"

τοῦτο: "this (fact)" i.e. that she is very white

ἢν μὴ ἐπιπρέπῃ: pr. subj. in pr. gen. protasis, "*unless there is visible in addition* also some red"

Present General Conditions

A present general condition has ἐάν (Attic ἤν) + subj. in the protasis; present indicative in the apodosis:

οὐκ ἐπαινεῖται δὲ τοῦτο, ἢν μὴ ἐπιπρέπῃ: "For this is not praised, unless there is visible in addition"

However, Lucian sometimes uses the optative in the protasis of such conditions, especially when the premise is unlikely to be fulfilled:

εἴ ποτε γαλήνη εἴη ... ἐς τὸ ὕδωρ ἰδέ: "If ever there is calm, look in the water"

φορητόν (sc. ἐστι), καὶ εἰς λέοντα δὲ εἰ ἀλλαγείης. "It is bearable even if you were changed into a lion."

ΓΑΛΑΤΕΙΑ: Καὶ μὴν ἐγὼ μὲν ἡ ἀκράτως λευκὴ ὅμως ἐραστὴν ἔχω κἂν τοῦτον, ὑμῶν δὲ οὐκ ἔστιν ἥντινα ἢ ποιμὴν ἢ ναύτης ἢ πορθμεὺς ἐπαινεῖ· ὁ δέ γε Πολύφημος τά τε ἄλλα καὶ μουσικός ἐστι.

ΔΩΡΙΣ: Σιώπα, ὦ Γαλάτεια· ἠκούσαμεν αὐτοῦ ᾄδοντος ὁπότε ἐκώμασε πρώην ἐπὶ σέ· Ἀφροδίτη φίλη, ὄνον ἄν τις ὀγκᾶσθαι ἔδοξε. καὶ αὐτὴ δὲ ἡ πηκτὶς οἵα; κρανίον ἐλάφου γυμνὸν τῶν σαρκῶν, καὶ τὰ μὲν κέρατα πήχεις ὥσπερ ἦσαν, ζυγώσας δὲ αὐτὰ καὶ ἐνάψας τὰ νεῦρα, οὐδὲ

ᾄδω: to sing
ἀκούω: to hear (+ *gen. of source*)
ἄκρατος, -ον: unmixed, completely
Ἀφροδίτη, ἡ: Aphrodite
γυμνός, -ή, -όν: naked (+ *gen.*)
ἔλαφος, ὁ: a deer
ἐνάπτω: to bind on or to
ἐραστής, -οῦ, ὁ: a lover
ζυγόω: to yoke together
κέρας, -ατος, τό: a horn
κρανίον, τό: a skull
κωμάζω: to revel, make merry
λευκός, -ή, -όν: light, white, brilliant
μουσικός, -ή, -όν: of or for music, musical
ναύτης, -ου, ὁ: a sailor
νεῦρον, τό: a sinew, tendon
ὀγκάομαι: to bray
ὅμως: nevertheless
ὄνος, ὁ: an ass
ὁπότε: when
πηκτίς, -ίδος, ἡ: a harp
πῆχυς, ὁ: a handle (of a lyre)
ποιμήν, -ένος, ὁ: a herdsman
πορθμεύς, -έως, ὁ: a ferryman
πρῶος, -η, -ον: early
σάρξ, σαρκός, ἡ: flesh
σιωπάω: to be silent
φίλος, -η, -ον: loved, beloved, dear

καὶ μὴν: indicating disagreement, "and yet"
ἡ ἀκράτως λευκή: an attributive phrase, "I, the completely white one"
κἂν (=καὶ ἐάν) τοῦτον: "even if (I have) this one"
οὐκ ἔστιν ἥντινα: "there is no one of you whom"
γε: emphatic, "but *this very* Polyphemus"
τά τε ἄλλα καὶ: "is *other things and also*," i.e. "is especially"
σιώπα: pr. imper., "be silent!"
αὐτοῦ ᾄδοντος: pr. part. gen. after ἠκούσαμεν, "we heard *him singing*"
πρώην (sc. ἡμέραν): acc. of duration, "all morning long"
Ἀφροδίτη: "my dear Aphrodite" ironic
ἄν ... ἔδοξεν: aor. contrafactual, "someone might have imagined" + inf.
ὀγκᾶσθαι: pr. inf. complementing ἔδοξεν, "that he was braying"
τῶν σαρκῶν: gen. of separation after γυμνόν, "naked *of flesh*"
πήχεις ὥσπερ: "were *sort of handles*"
ζυγώσας: aor. part., "having yoked together"
ἐνάψας: aor. part., "having bound"

Lucian

κόλλοπι περιστρέψας, ἐμελῴδει ἄμουσόν τι καὶ ἀπῳδόν, ἄλλο μὲν αὐτὸς βοῶν, ἄλλο δὲ ἡ λύρα ὑπήχει, ὥστε οὐδὲ κατέχειν τὸν γέλωτα ἐδυνάμεθα ἐπὶ τῷ ἐρωτικῷ ἐκείνῳ ᾄσματι· ἡ μὲν γὰρ Ἠχὼ οὐδὲ ἀποκρίνεσθαι αὐτῷ ἤθελεν οὕτω λάλος οὖσα βρυχομένῳ, ἀλλ' ᾐσχύνετο, εἰ φανείη μιμουμένη τραχεῖαν ᾠδὴν καὶ καταγέλαστον. ἔφερε δὲ ὁ

αἰσχύνομαι: to be ashamed
ἄμουσος, -ον: unrefined, inelegant
ἀποκρίνομαι: to answer, respond to (+ *dat*.)
ἀπῳδός, -όν: out of tune
ᾆσμα, -ατος, τό: a song
βοάω: to cry aloud, to shout
βρυχω: to gnash ones's teeth
γέλως, -ωτος, ὁ: laughter
δύναμαι: to be able, capable
ἐθέλω: to will, wish to (+ *inf*.)
ἐρωτικός, -ή, -όν: amatory
καταγέλαστος, ον: ridiculous, laughable

κατέχω: to hold fast, restrain
κόλλοψ, -οπος, ὁ: a peg or screw
λάλος, -ον: talkative, loquacious
λύρα, ἡ: a lyre
μελῳδέω: to sing, chant
μιμέομαι: to mimic, imitate, represent
περιστρέφω: to twist round (+ *dat*.)
τραχύς, -εῖα, -ύ: rugged, rough
ὑπηχέω: to sound in answer, respond
φαίνομαι: to seem to (+ *part*.)
ᾠδή, ἡ: a song, lay, ode

περιστρέψας: aor. part., "not *having twisted around*" + dat.
ἄλλο μὲν ... ἄλλο δὲ: "one thing ... something else"
ὥστε ... ἐδυνάμεθα: res. cl., "so that we were unable"
κατέχειν: compl. infin. after ἐδυνάμεθα, "unable *to contain*"
Ἠχὼ: Echo, the nymph who could only copy the voice of others
ἀποκρίνεσθαι: pr. inf. complementing ἤθελεν, "wish *to answer*"
ἤθελεν: impf. in past general apodosis, "she would not want to" + inf.
λάλος οὖσα: pr. part. concessive, "*even though being* talkative"
βρυχομένῳ: pr. part. mod. αὐτῷ, circumstantial, "when he is gnashing (his teeth)"
ᾐσχύνετο: impf. in past general apodosis, "she would be ashamed"
εἰ φανείη: aor. opt. pass. in past general protasis, "if (ever) she seemed to" + part.
μιμουμένη: pr. part. supplementing φανείη, "seemed *to be imitating*"

Translating Participles

Greek has many more participles than English. The aorist participle is quite common and has no parallel in English in most cases. Our "translationese" versions of aorist participles will often sound like perfect participles (*παραλαβοῦσα*: "having taken her along") because English has no way to indicate simple time with a participle. More idiomatic in these cases would be some kind of periphrasis, such as "once he had taken her along," but our translationese version will indicate the syntactic relations more clearly.

ἐπέραστος ἐν ταῖς ἀγκάλαις ἀθυρμάτιον ἄρκτου σκύλακα τὸ λάσιον αὐτῷ προσεοικότα. τίς οὐκ ἂν φθονήσειέ σοι, ὦ Γαλάτεια, τοιούτου ἐραστοῦ;

ΓΑΛΑΤΕΙΑ: Οὐκοῦν σύ, Δωρί, δεῖξον ἡμῖν τὸν σεαυτῆς, καλλίω δῆλον ὅτι ὄντα καὶ ᾠδικώτερον καὶ κιθαρίζειν ἄμεινον ἐπιστάμενον.

ΔΩΡΙΣ: Ἀλλὰ ἐραστὴς μὲν οὐδεὶς ἔστι μοι οὐδὲ σεμνύνομαι ἐπέραστος εἶναι· τοιοῦτος δὲ οἷος ὁ Κύκλωψ ἐστί,

---

ἀγκάλη, ἡ: an arm
ἀθυρμάτιον, τό: a plaything, pet
ἀμείνων, -ον: better
ἄρκτος, ἡ: a bear
δείκνυμι: to bring to light, display, exhibit
δῆλος, -ον: visible, conspicuous
ἐπέραστος, -ον: lovely, amiable
ἐπίσταμαι: to know how to (+ inf.)
ἐραστής, -οῦ, ὁ: a lover
κιθαρίζω: to play the cithara, to be educated

Κύκλωψ, -ωπος, ὁ: a Cyclops
λάσιος, -ον: hairy, rough
οὐκοῦν: therefore, then, accordingly
προσέοικα: to be like, resemble (+ dat.)
σεμνύνομαι: to be proud to (+ inf.)
σκύλαξ, ὁ: a cub
τοιοῦτος, -αύτη, -οῦτο: such as this
φθονέω: to be envious of X (dat.) about Y (gen.)
ᾠδικός, -ή, -όν: fond of singing, vocal

τὸ λάσιον: acc. resp., "like him *in roughness*"
προσεοικότα: perf. part., "resembling" + dat.
ἂν φθονήσειε: aor. opt. pot., "would anyone envy you?"
δεῖξον: aor. imper., "show!"
τὸν σεαυτῆς (sc. ἐραστήν): "show *your own lover*"
καλλίω (=καλλίο(ν)α): acc. pred. after ὄντα, "being *more handsome*"
δῆλον ὅτι ὄντα: pr. part. representing δῆλον ὅτι ἐστι, "clearly being"
κιθαρίζειν: pr. inf. expex. after ἐπιστάμενον, "more skilled *at playing the cithara*"
τοιοῦτος δὲ οἷος: correlatives, "such a one as"

Potential Optatives

The optative with ἄν expresses potentiality, with a range of possible meanings:

τίς οὐκ ἂν φθονήσειέ σοι: "would anyone envy you?"

ἡδέως ἂν μάθοιμι παρὰ σοῦ: "I would like to learn from you."

καὶ τίς ἂν ἡ ἀπάτη ... γένοιτο; "What deception could there be?"

Lucian

κινάβρας ἀπόζων ὥσπερ ὁ τράγος, ὠμοφάγος, ὥς φασι, καὶ σιτούμενος τοὺς ἐπιδημοῦντας τῶν ξένων, σοὶ γένοιτο καὶ πάντοτε σὺ ἀντερῴης αὐτοῦ.

ἀντεράω: to love in return
ἀπόζω: to smell of (+ gen.)
ἐπιδημέω: to visit
κινάβρα, ἡ: the smell of a goat
ξένος, ὁ: a foreigner

πάντοτε: at all times, always
σιτέω: to take food, eat
τράγος ὁ: a he-goat
ὠμοφάγος, -ον: eating raw flesh

κινάβρας: gen. after ἀπόζων, "smelling *of a goat*"
τοὺς ἐπιδημοῦντας: pr. part., "those visiting"
τῶν ξένων: partitive gen., "of strangers"
γένοιτο: aor. opt. wish for the future, "may he be"
ἀντερῴης: pr. opt. wish for the future, "may you love him" + gen.

Imperatives

There are many more imperatives in dialogues, so it is worth reviewing their forms. Here is the regular conjugation of the present and first aorist illustrated with λύω:

Present Imperative

Number	Person	Active	Middle / Passive
Singular	2nd	λῦε	λύου (from ε-σο)
	3rd	λυέτω	λυέσθω
Plural	2nd	λύετε	λύεσθε
	3rd	λυόντων	λυέσθων

Aorist Imperative

Number	Person	Active	Middle	Passive
Singular	2nd	λῦσον	λύσαι	λύθητι
	3rd	λυσάτω	λυσάσθω	λυθήτω
Plural	2nd	λύσατε	λύσασθε	λύθητε
	3rd	λυσάντων	λυσάσθων	λυθέντων

The imperatives of second aorist verbs regularly take the same endings as the present imperative: λάβε, λαβέτω, etc.

The perfect imperative is rare, but note τεθάφθω, the 3rd. sing. perf. imper. of θάπτω, "let her be buried."

2. The Cyclops and Poseidon

The subject of this dialogue is the encounter between Odysseus and the Cyclops in Odyssey 9, also treated in Euripides' Cyclops. Polyphemus complains to his father about his treatment at the hands of Odysseus, giving his own version of the story, with some prodding about details from Poseidon. Poseidon hints at his revenge on Odysseus in the final lines, but Poseidon also seems to find the story a bit amusing.

ΚΥΚΛΩΨ: Ὦ πάτερ, οἷα πέπονθα ὑπὸ τοῦ καταράτου ξένου, ὃς μεθύσας ἐξετύφλωσέ με κοιμωμένῳ ἐπιχειρήσας.

ΠΟΣΕΙΔΩΝ: Τίς δὲ ἦν ὁ ταῦτα τολμήσας, ὦ Πολύφημε;

ΚΥΚΛΩΨ: Τὸ μὲν πρῶτον Οὖτιν ἑαυτὸν ἀπεκάλει, ἐπεὶ δὲ διέφυγε καὶ ἔξω ἦν βέλους, Ὀδυσσεὺς ὀνομάζεσθαι ἔφη.

ἀποκαλέω: to call
βέλος, -ους, τό: a missile, something thrown
διαφεύγω: to flee through, get away from, escape
ἐκτυφλόω: to blind
ἔξω: outside of (+ *gen.*)
ἐπιχειρέω: to lay hands upon (+ *dat.*)
κατάρατος, -ον: accursed, abominable
κοιμάομαι: to fall sleep

μεθύσκω: to make drunk, intoxicate, inebriate
Ὀδυσσεύς, -έως, οἱ: Odysseus
οἷος, οἵα, οἷον: such as, what sort of
ὀνομάζω: to name
οὖτις, οὖτι: no one, nothing
πάσχω: to suffer
πατήρ, πατρός, ὁ: a father
τολμάω: to undertake, dare

οἷα: exclamation, "*what things* I have suffered!"
πέπονθα: perf. of πάσχω, "I have suffered"
μεθύσας: aor. part., "having made me drunk"
κοιμωμένῳ: pr. part. dat. agreeing with obj. of ἐπιχειρήσας (*μοι*), "having laid hands on me *while sleeping*"
ὁ τολμήσας: aor. part., "the one who dared"
τὸ πρῶτον: adv. acc., "at first"
Οὖτιν: acc. s., "Nobody," the name Odysseus gives in the episode.
ἀπεκάλει: impf., "he kept calling himself"
διέφυγε: aor., "when *he fled*"
ὀνομάζεσθαι: pres. infin. pass. in ind. st., "said *that he was named*"

ΠΟΣΕΙΔΩΝ: Οἶδα ὃν λέγεις, τὸν Ἰθακήσιον· ἐξ Ἰλίου δ' ἀνέπλει. ἀλλὰ πῶς ταῦτα ἔπραξεν οὐδὲ πάνυ εὐθαρσὴς ὤν;

ἀναπλέω: to sail up, to go up stream
εὐθαρσής, -ές: of good courage
Ἰθακήσιος, -ον: from Ithaca
Ἴλιος, ὁ: Ilium, the city of Troy

οἶδα: to know
πάνυ: altogether, entirely, too
πράττω: to do
πῶς: how? in what way or manner?

ἔπραξεν: aor., "how *did he do* these things?
ὤν: pr. part. concessive, "despite not *being*"

Participles: General Principles

Participles fall into three broad classes of use, with many other distinctions:

1. Attributive participles modify a noun or pronoun like other adjectives. They can occur with an article in the attributive position or with no article:

    Τίς δὲ ἦν ὁ ταῦτα τολμήσας: "Who is *the one who dared?*"

    σιτούμενος τοὺς ἐπιδημοῦντας: "eating *those who are visiting*"

2. Circumstantial participles are added to a noun or pronoun to set forth some circumstance under which an action takes place. Although agreeing with a noun or pronoun, these participles actually qualify the verb in a sentence, indicating time, manner, means, cause, purpose, concession, condition or attendant circumstance. Circumstantial participles can occur in the genitive absolute construction.

    ἀλλὰ τὴν σκευὴν ἀναλαβόντα με καὶ ᾄσαντα θρῆνόν τινα ἐπ' ἐμαυτῷ ἑκόντα ἐάσατε ῥῖψαι ἐμαυτόν: "but allow me willingly to throw myself, (me) *having taken* up my equipment and *having sung* a dirge over myself."

    For more examples, see p. 29.

3. Supplementary participles complete the idea of certain verbs. Often it is the participle itself that expresses the main action:

    ὑπερεώρας καὶ ἔχαιρες λυπῶν αὐτήν: "you despised her and enjoyed *grieving* her."

    εἰ φανείη μιμουμένη τραχεῖαν ᾠδήν: "if ever she seemed *to be imitating* that rough song."

The participial form of indirect discourse after verbs of showing and perceiving is a special class of supplementary participles.

    ἔδειξεν πολὺν ἄγων χρυσόν τε καὶ ἄργυρον: "he revealed *that he was leading* gold and silver."

ΚΥΚΛΩΨ: Κατέλαβον ἐν τῷ ἄντρῳ ἀπὸ τῆς νομῆς ἀναστρέψας πολλούς τινας, ἐπιβουλεύοντας δῆλον ὅτι τοῖς ποιμνίοις· ἐπεὶ γὰρ ἐπέθηκα τῇ θύρᾳ τὸ πῶμα — πέτρα δέ ἐστί παμμεγέθης — καὶ τὸ πῦρ ἀνέκαυσα ἐναυσάμενος ὃ ἔφερον δένδρον ἀπὸ τοῦ ὄρους, ἐφάνησαν ἀποκρύπτειν αὐτοὺς πειρώμενοι· ἐγὼ δὲ συλλαβών τινας αὐτῶν, ὥσπερ εἰκὸς ἦν, κατέφαγον λῃστάς γε ὄντας. ἐνταῦθα ὁ πανουργότατος ἐκεῖνος, εἴτε Οὖτις εἴτε

ἀνακαίω: to light up
ἀναστρέφω: to turn upside down, upset
ἀποκρύπτω: to hide from, keep hidden from
δένδρον, τό: a tree
δῆλος, -ον: visible, clear
εἰκός: reasonable
ἐναύω: to get a light
ἐπιβουλεύω: to plan or contrive against (+ dat.)
ἐπιτίθημι: to place X (acc.) on Y (dat.)
θύρα, ἡ: a door
καταλαμβάνω: to seize upon, lay hold of
κατεσθίω: to eat up, devour

λῃστής, -οῦ, ὁ: a robber, plunderer
νομή, ἡ: a pasture
ὄρος, -ους, τό: a mountain, hill
παμμεγέθης, -ες: very large
πάνουργος -ον: devious
πειράω: to attempt, try (+ *inf.*)
πέτρα, ἡ: a rock
ποίμνιον, τό: a flock
πῦρ, τό: fire
πῶμα, τό: a lid, stopper
συλλαμβάνω: to collect, gather together
φαίνομαι: to appear, to seem
φέρω: to bear

κατέλαβον: aor., "I seized them"
ἀναστρέψας: aor. part., "*having driven* them from the pasture"
δῆλον ὅτι: "it is clear that" + part., i.e. *clearly* contriving against" + dat.
ἐπέθηκα: aor. of ἐπιτίθημι, "I placed upon"
τῇ θύρᾳ: "upon *the door*"
ἀνέκαυσα: aor. of ἀνακαίω, "*I lit* the fire"
ἐναυσάμενος: aor. part. instr. of ἐν-αύω, "*by having got a light* from the tree""
ὃ ἔφερον: "which I was carrying"
ἐφάνησαν: aor. pass., "they seemed to" + part.
ἀποκρύπτειν: pr. inf., "trying *to hide* themselves"
αὐτοὺς: =ἑαυτοὺς, "themselves"
συλλαβών: aor. part. of συν-λαμβάνω, "having gathered"
κατέφαγον: aor. of κατα-ἐσθίω, "I devoured"
λῃστάς: pred. acc. after ὄντας, "since they were *robbers*"
εἴτε... εἴτε: "whether...or"

Ὀδυσσεὺς ἦν, δίδωσί μοι πιεῖν φάρμακόν τι ἐγχέας, ἡδὺ μὲν καὶ εὔοσμον, ἐπιβουλότατον δὲ καὶ ταραχωδέστατον· ἅπαντα γὰρ εὐθὺς ἐδόκει μοι περιφέρεσθαι πιόντι καὶ τὸ σπήλαιον αὐτὸ ἀνεστρέφετο καὶ οὐκέτι ὅλως ἐν ἐμαυτοῦ ἤμην, τέλος δὲ εἰς ὕπνον κατεσπάσθην. ὁ δὲ ἀποξύνας τὸν μοχλὸν καὶ πυρώσας γε προσέτι ἐτύφλωσέ με καθεύδοντα, καὶ ἀπ' ἐκείνου τυφλός εἰμί σοι, ὦ Πόσειδον.

ἀναστρέφω: to turn upside down, upset
ἅπας, ἅπασα, ἅπαν: all, every, whole
ἀποξύνω: to bring to a point, make taper
δίδωμι: to give
ἐγχέω: to pour out
ἐπίβουλος, -ον: plotting against, treacherous
εὔοσμος, -ον: sweet-smelling, fragrant
ἡδύς, -εῖα, -ύ: sweet
καθεύδω: to lie down to sleep, sleep
κατοσπάω: to drag down
μοχλός, ὁ: a bar
ὅλως: adv. entirely
οὐκέτι: no more, no longer

περιφέρω: to carry round
πίνω: to drink
πίνω: to drink
Ποσειδῶν, -ῶνος, ὁ: Poseidon
προσέτι: over and above, besides
πυρόω: to burn with fire, burn up
σπήλαιον, τό: a grotto, cave, cavern
ταραχώδης, -ες: troublous, turbulent
τέλος: adv. finally
τυφλός, -ή, -όν: blind
τυφλόω: to blind, make blind
ὕπνος, ὁ: sleep, slumber
φάρμακον, τό: a drug, medicine

πιεῖν: aor. inf. of purpose after δίδωσί, "he gives me *to drink*"
ἐγχέας: aor. part. of ἐν-χέω, "having poured out"
περιφέρεσθαι: pr. inf. pass. of περιφέρω, complementing ἐδόκει, "seemed *to be carried around*" i.e. to be spinning
πιόντι: aor. part. dat., "to me *having drunk*"
ἤμην: impf. of εἰμί, "I was no longer in myself" i.e. in control of myself
κατεσπάσθην: aor. pass. of κατα-σπάω, "I was dragged down"
ἀποξύνας: aor. part., "having sharpened"
ἀπ' ἐκείνου (sc. χρόνου): "from that time"

ΠΟΣΕΙΔΩΝ: Ὡς βαθὺν ἐκοιμήθης, ὦ τέκνον, ὃς οὐκ ἐξέθορες μεταξὺ τυφλούμενος. ὁ δ᾽ οὖν Ὀδυσσεὺς πῶς διέφυγεν; οὐ γὰρ ἂν εὖ οἶδ᾽ ὅτι ἠδυνήθη ἀποκινῆσαι τὴν πέτραν ἀπὸ τῆς θύρας.

ΚΥΚΛΩΨ: Ἀλλ᾽ ἐγὼ ἀφεῖλον, ὡς μᾶλλον αὐτὸν λάβοιμι ἐξιόντα, καὶ καθίσας παρὰ τὴν θύραν ἐθήρων τὰς χεῖρας ἐκπετάσας, μόνα παρεὶς τὰ πρόβατα εἰς τὴν νομήν, ἐντειλάμενος τῷ κριῷ ὁπόσα ἐχρῆν πράττειν αὐτὸν ὑπὲρ ἐμοῦ.

ἀποκινέω: to move away from
ἀφαιρέω: to take away from, left
βαθύς, -εῖα, -ύ: deep or high
διαφεύγω: to get away from, escape
δύναμαι: to be able, capable
ἐκθρῴσκω: to leap forth
ἐκπετάννυμι: to spread out
ἐντέλλω: to enjoin, command (+ *dat.*)
θηράω: to hunt or chase
θύρα, ἡ: a door
καθίζω: to make to sit down, seat
κοιμάω: to lull or hush to sleep, put to sleep
κριός, ὁ: a ram
λαμβάνω: to take
μόνος, -η, -ον: alone
νομή, ἡ: a pasture, pasturage
οἶδα: to know
παρίημι: to disregard, allow past
πέτρα, ἡ: a rock
πράττω: to do
πρόβατα, τά: sheep
πῶς: how? in what way or manner?
τέκνον, τό: a child
τυφλόω: to blind, make blind
χείρ, χειρός, ἡ: a hand
χρή: it is necessary

ἐκοιμήθης: aor. pass., "you have been put to sleep"
ἐξέθορες: aor. of ἐκθρῴσκω, "you who did not spring forth"
μεταξὺ τυφλούμενος: pr. part., "in the midst of being blinded"
διέφυγεν: aor., "how *did he flee?*"
εὖ οἶδ᾽ ὅτι: parenthetical, "I know that well"
ἂν ... ἠδυνήθη: aor. pass. contrafactual, "he would not have been able to" + inf.
ἀποκινῆσαι: aor. inf. complementing ἠδυνήθη, "able *to move away*
ἀφεῖλον: aor. of ἀπο-αἱρέω, "I removed it"
ὡς ... λάβοιμι: aor. opt. in purp. cl., "in order to catch him"
ἐξιόντα: pr. part. acc., "him *going out*"
καθίσας: aor. part., "I *having sat down*"
ἐθήρων: impf., "I was hunting him"
ἐκπετάσας: aor. part. inst., "*by having spread out* my hands"
παρεὶς: aor. part. of παρα-ἵημι, "having let pass"
ἐντειλάμενος: aor. part., "having commanded" + dat.
ἐχρῆν: impf. of χρή in ind. com., "commanded *what things were necessary*" + inf.

ΠΟΣΕΙΔΩΝ: Μανθάνω· ὑπ' ἐκείνοις ἔλαθον ὑπεξελθόντες· σὲ δὲ τοὺς ἄλλους Κύκλωπας ἔδει ἐπιβοήσασθαι ἐπ' αὐτόν.

ΚΥΚΛΩΨ: Συνεκάλεσα, ὦ πάτερ, καὶ ἧκον· ἐπεὶ δὲ ἤροντο τοῦ ἐπιβουλεύοντος τοὔνομα κἀγὼ ἔφην ὅτι «Οὖτίς ἐστι,» μελαγχολᾶν οἰηθέντες με ᾤχοντο ἀπιόντες. οὕτω κατεσοφίσατό με ὁ κατάρατος τῷ ὀνόματι. καὶ ὃ μάλιστα ἠνίασέ με, ὅτι καὶ ὀνειδίζων ἐμοὶ τὴν συμφοράν, «Οὐδὲ ὁ πατήρ,» φησίν, «ὁ Ποσειδῶν ἰάσεται σε.»

ἀνιάω: to grieve, distress
ἀπέρχομαι: to go away
ἐπιβοάω: to call upon or to, cry out to
ἐπιβουλεύω: to plan or contrive against
ἐρωτάω: to ask, enquire
ἥκω: to have come, be present
ἰάομαι: to heal, cure
κατάρατος, -ον: accursed, abominable
κατασοφίζομαι: to outwit
λανθάνω: to escape notice (+ part.)
μανθάνω: to learn

μελαγχολάω: to be mad from black bile
οἴμαι: to suppose, think
οἴχομαι: to be gone, to leave
ὀνειδίζω: to reproach X (dat.) for Y (acc.)
ὄνομα, τό: a name
οὖτις, -τις: no one or nobody
πατήρ, πατρός, ὁ: a father
συγκαλέω: to call to together
συμφορά, ἡ: an event, disaster
ὑπεξέρχομαι: to go out secretly

ἔλαθον: aor. of λανθάνω, "they escaped your notice" + part.
ὑπεξελθόντες: aor. part. suppl. ἔλαθον, "having gone out"
ἔδει: impf., "it was necessary" + inf.
ἐπιβοήσασθαι: aor. inf. of ἐπιβοάω, "necessary that you *call upon*"
συνεκάλεσα: aor. of συν-καλέω, "I did call them."
ἧκον: impf., "they were coming"
ἤροντο: aor. of ἐρωτάω, "when *they asked*"
τοῦ ἐπιβουλεύοντος: gen., "the name *of the one contriving against*"
τοὔνομα: = τό ὄνομα, "the name"
κἀγὼ: = καὶ + ἐγώ, "and I"
μελαγχολᾶν: pr. inf. in ind. st. after οἰηθέντες, "having supposed me *to be mad*"
οἰηθέντες: aor. pass. part. of οἶμαι with act. meaning, "having supposed"
ᾤχοντο: impf. of οἴχομαι, "they left."
ἀπιόντες: pr. part. of ἀπο-ἔρχομαι, "going away"
τῷ ὀνόματι: dat. of means, "by the name."
ἰάσεταί: fut. of ἰάομαι, "will cure you"

Dialogues of the Sea Gods

ΠΟΣΕΙΔΩΝ: Θάρρει, ὦ τέκνον· ἀμυνοῦμαι γὰρ αὐτόν, ὡς μάθῃ ὅτι, καὶ εἰ πήρωσίν μοι τῶν ὀφθαλμῶν ἰᾶσθαι ἀδύνατον, τὰ γοῦν τῶν πλεόντων τὸ σῴζειν αὐτοὺς καὶ ἀπολλύναι ἐπ' ἐμοί ἐστι· πλεῖ δὲ ἔτι.

The Blinding of Polyphemus, krater fragment, 7th century BCE (Argos Archaeological Museum, Greece)

ἀδύνατος, -ον: unable
ἀμύνω: to keep off, ward off
ἀπόλλυμι: to destroy utterly, kill, slay
γοῦν: at least then, at any rate
θαρρέω: to be of good courage, take courage

μόνος, -η, -ον: alone
πήρωσις, -εως, ἡ: a being maimed, mutilation
πλέω: to sail, go by sea
σῴζω; to save
τέκνον, τό: a child

θάρρει: imp. of θαρρέω, "have courage!"
ἀμυνοῦμαι: fut., "I will ward him off"
ὡς μάθῃ: aor. subj. in purp. cl., "so that he will learn"
ὅτι ... ἐπ' ἐμοί ἐστι: the apodosis of a simple cond. in ind. st., "that are in my power"
καὶ εἰ ... ἀδύνατον (sc. ἐστι): protasis of simple cond., "even if it is impossible for me to" + inf.
ἰᾶσθαι: pr. inf. epex. after ἀδύνατον, "impossible *to cure*"
τὰ γοῦν τῶν πλεόντων: subj. of ἐστι, "*the concerns of those sailing* are in my power"
τὸ σῴζειν καὶ ἀπολλύναι: pr. inf. artic. in apposition to τά: "namely, the saving and destroying"
πλεῖ δὲ ἔτι: "and he is still sailing"

3. Poseidon and Alpheus

The story of the river Alpheus and his beloved Arethusa, who is an Arcadian spring in Syracuse, is recounted in a number of ancient sources, mostly with erotic overtones. The river is imagined flowing under the Ionian Sea and reemerging unaffected by the seawater in Sicily. In Lucian's dialogue Poseidon questions Alpheus about the details of his long distance affair, but Alpheus is in a hurry and cuts the conversation short.

ΠΟΣΕΙΔΩΝ: Τί τοῦτο, ὦ Ἀλφειέ; μόνος τῶν ἄλλων ἐμπεσὼν ἐς τὸ πέλαγος οὔτε ἀναμίγνυσαι τῇ ἅλμῃ, ὡς ἔθος ποταμοῖς ἅπασιν, οὔτε ἀναπαύεις σεαυτὸν διαχυθείς, ἀλλὰ διὰ τῆς θαλάττης ξυνεστὼς καὶ γλυκὺ φυλάττων τὸ ῥεῖθρον, ἀμιγὴς ἔτι καὶ καθαρὸς ἐπείγῃ οὐκ οἶδ' ὅπου

ἅλμη, ἡ: seawater, brine
Ἀλφειός, ὁ: Alpheus
ἀμιγής, -ές: unmixed
ἀναμίγνυμι: to mingle
ἀναπαύω: to make to halt, to rest
γλυκύς, -εῖα, -ύ: sweet
διαχέω: to pour different ways, to disperse
ἔθος, ὁ: a custom, law
ἐμπίπτω: to fall into
ἐπείγομαι: to press forward, urge on
θάλαττα, ἡ: the sea
καθαρός, -α, -ον: clean, pure
ξυνίστημι: to set together, combine, unite
πέλαγος, -ους, τό: a sea
ποταμός, ὁ: a river, stream
ῥεῖθρον, τό: a river, stream
φυλάττω: to guard, keep safe

τῶν ἄλλων: gen., "of the other (rivers)"
ἐμπεσών: aor. part., "having fallen"
ἀναμίγνυσαι: pr. mid. 2 s., "you neither mingle with" + dat.
ποταμοῖς ἅπασιν: dat., "the custom *to all the rivers*"
διαχυθείς: aor. pass. part. instrumental of δια-χέω, "by dispersing yourself."
ξυνεστώς: perf. part. of ξυν-ἵστημι, "having remained composed"
γλυκὺ: acc. pred., "keeping your flow *sweet*"
ἐπείγῃ: pr. mid., "you press forward"
οὐκ οἶδ' ὅπου: parenthetical, "I don't know where"

βύθιος ὑποδὺς καθάπερ οἱ λάροι καὶ ἐρωδιοί· καὶ ἔοικας ἀνακύψειν που καὶ αὖθις ἀναφανεῖν σεαυτόν.

ΑΛΦΕΙΟΣ: Ἐρωτικόν τι τὸ πρᾶγμά ἐστιν, ὦ Πόσειδον, ὥστε μὴ ἔλεγχε· ἠράσθης δὲ καὶ αὐτὸς πολλάκις.

ΠΟΣΕΙΔΩΝ: Γυναικός, ὦ Ἀλφειέ, ἢ νύμφης ἐρᾷς ἢ καὶ τῶν Νηρηΐδων αὐτῶν μιᾶς;

ΑΛΦΕΙΟΣ: Οὔκ, ἀλλὰ πηγῆς, ὦ Πόσειδον.

ΠΟΣΕΙΔΩΝ: Ἡ δὲ ποῦ σοι γῆς αὕτη ῥεῖ;

ΑΛΦΕΙΟΣ: Νησιῶτίς ἐστι Σικελή· Ἀρέθουσαν αὐτὴν καλοῦσιν.

ἀνακύπτω: to lift up the head, arise
ἀναφαίνω: to show
Ἀρέθουσα, ἡ: Arethusa
αὖθις: back, back again
βύθιος, -α, -ον: in the deep, sunken
γῆ, ἡ: land
γυνή, -αίκος, ἡ: a woman
εἷς, μία, ἕν: one
ἐλέγχω: to accuse, test, examine
ἔοικα: to seem, to be likely (+ inf.)
ἐράω: to love, to be in love with
ἐρωτικός, -ή, -όν: amatory
ἐρῳδιός, ὁ: a heron

καθάπερ: just as
καλέω: to call, name
λάρος, ὁ: a cormorant
Νηρηίς, -ίδος, ἡ: a Nereid
νησιώτης, -ου, ὁ: an islander
νύμφη, ἡ: a nymph
πηγή, ἡ: running waters, streams
πολλάκις: many times, often
πρᾶγμα, -ατος, τό: a matter
ῥέω: to flow, run, stream, gush
Σικελός, -ή, -όν: Sicilian
ὑποδύω: to plunge down
ὥστε: and so

ὑποδὺς: aor. part., "having plunged down"
ἀνακύψειν: fut. inf. complementing ἔοικας, "you are likely *to rise up*"
ἀναφανεῖν: fut. inf. also complementing ἔοικας, "and to show yourself"
μὴ ἔλεγχε: pr. imper. in prohibition, "do not accuse!"
ἠράσθης: aor. pass. of ἐράω, "you have been in love."
γυναικός: gen. after ἐρᾷς, "do you love *a woman*?"
πηγῆς: gen. after ἐράω understood, "I love *a fountain*"
ἡ δὲ: "but she"

ΠΟΣΕΙΔΩΝ: Οἶδα οὐκ ἄμορφον, ὦ Ἀλφειέ, τὴν Ἀρέθουσαν, ἀλλὰ διαυγής ἐστι καὶ διὰ καθαροῦ ἀναβλύζει καὶ τὸ ὕδωρ ἐπιπρέπει ταῖς ψηφῖσιν ὅλον ὑπὲρ αὐτῶν φαινόμενον ἀργυροειδές.

ΑΛΦΕΙΟΣ: Ὡς ἀληθῶς οἶσθα τὴν πηγήν, ὦ Πόσειδον· παρ' ἐκείνην οὖν ἀπέρχομαι.

ΠΟΣΕΙΔΩΝ: Ἀλλ' ἄπιθι μὲν καὶ εὐτύχει ἐν τῷ ἔρωτι· ἐκεῖνο δέ μοι εἰπέ, ποῦ τὴν Ἀρέθουσαν εἶδες αὐτὸς μὲν Ἀρκὰς ὤν, ἡ δὲ ἐν Συρακούσαις ἐστίν;

ΑΛΦΕΙΟΣ: Ἐπειγόμενόν με κατέχεις, ὦ Πόσειδον, περίεργα ἐρωτῶν.

ἀληθῶς: honestly, truly
ἄμορφος, -ον: misshapen, unsightly
ἀναβλύζω: to spout up
ἀπέρχομαι: to go away, depart from
ἀργυροειδής, -ές: like silver, silvery
Ἀρκὰς, ὁ: an Arcadian
διαυγής, -ές: transparent
εἶπον: to speak, say
ἐπείγομαι: to press forward, hasten
ἐπιπρέπω: to be conspicuous on (+ *dat.*)
ἔρως, -ωτος, ὁ: love
ἐρωτάω: to question

εὐτυχέω: to be well off, prosperous
κατέχω: to hold fast
οἶδα: to know
οἶδα: to know
ὅλος, -η, -ον: whole, entire
περίεργος, -ον: superfluous
πηγή, ἡ: running waters, streams
ποῦ: where?
Συράκουσαι, αἱ: Syracuse
ὕδωρ, -ατος, τό: water
φαίνομαι: to appear
ψηφίς, -ῖδος, ἡ: a small pebble

διὰ καθαροῦ (sc. ὁδοῦ): "she spouts up *through a clear path*"
φαινόμενον: pr. part. agreeing with ὕδωρ, "water *appearing*"
ἄπιθι: pr. imper., "go!"
εὐτύχει: pr. imper., "be prosperous!"
ποῦ ... εἶδες: aor., "where did you see?"
ἐπειγόμενόν: pr. part., "me, *who am pressing forward*"

ΠΟΣΕΙΔΩΝ: Εὖ λέγεις: χώρει παρὰ τὴν ἀγαπωμένην, καὶ ἀναδὺς ἀπὸ τῆς θαλάττης ξυναυλίᾳ μίγνυσο τῇ πηγῇ καὶ ἓν ὕδωρ γίγνεσθε.

Alpheus and Arethusa, marble relief, c. 1560
(Florence, Museo Nazionale del Bargello)

ἀγαπάω: to treat with affection, love
ἀναδύω: to come to the top of water
εἷς, μία, ἕν: one
μίγνυμι: to mingle

ξυναυλία, ἡ: a living together
πηγή, ἡ: running waters, streams
ὕδωρ, -ατος, τό: water
χωρέω: to give way, draw back

χώρει: pr. imper., "go away!"
τὴν ἀγαπωμένην: acc., "to *your beloved*"
ἀναδὺς: aor. part., "*having come up* from the sea"
μίγνυσο: pr. imper. mid., "mingle with!" + dat.
γίγνεσθε: pr. imper., "*become* one water!"

4. Proteus and Menelaus

This dialogue takes its inspiration from Odyssey 4, where Menelaus recounts his capture of Proteus, who changes shape while the hero is holding him fast. Menelaus accuses Proteus of being a charlatan who merely appears to be changing form. The pseudo-scientific character of the exchange pokes fun at the improbabilities of the Homeric story.

ΜΕΝΕΛΑΟΣ: Ἀλλὰ ὕδωρ μέν σε γενέσθαι, ὦ Πρωτεῦ, οὐκ ἀπίθανον, ἐνάλιόν γε ὄντα, καὶ δένδρον, ἔτι φορητόν, καὶ εἰς λέοντα δὲ ὁπότε ἀλλαγείης, ὅμως οὐδὲ τοῦτο ἔξω πίστεως· εἰ δὲ καὶ πῦρ γίγνεσθαι δυνατὸν ἐν θαλάττῃ οἰκοῦντά σε, τοῦτο πάνυ θαυμάζω καὶ ἀπιστῶ.

ΠΡΩΤΕΥΣ: Μὴ θαυμάσῃς, ὦ Μενέλαε· γίγνομαι γάρ.

ἀλλάττω: to change, alter
ἀπίθανος, -ον: incredible, unlikely, improbable
ἀπιστέω: to disbelieve
δένδρον, τό: a tree
δυνατός, -ή, -όν: able to (+ *inf*.)
ἐνάλιος, -α, -ον: in, on, of the sea
ἔξω: outside of (+ *gen*.)
θαυμάζω: to wonder at

λέων, -οντος, ὁ: a lion
Μενέλαος, ὁ: Menelaus
οἰκέω: to inhabit, occupy
ὅμως: similarly
πίστις, -εως, ἡ: belief
πῦρ, τό: fire
ὕδωρ, -ατος, τό: water
φορητός: bearable

σε γενέσθαι: aor. inf. in ind. st. after ἀπίθανον (sc. ἐστι), "it is not incredible *that you become*"
ὄντα: pr. part. causal, "*since you are* of the sea"
δένδρον: pred. acc. also after γενέσθαι, "that you become *a tree*"
ἔτι φορητόν (sc. ἐστι): "it is also bearable"
ἀλλαγείης: aor. opt. pass. in gen. temp. cl., "*whenever you are changed* into a lion"
εἰ ... δυνατὸν (sc. ἐστι): ind. quest. after θαυμάζω, " I wonder *whether it is possible*" + inf.
οἰκοῦντά: pr. part. acc. concessive, agreeing with σε, the subj. of γίγνεσθαι, "possible for you, *although living in the sea*, to become"
τοῦτο: "this," referring to the previous clause
μὴ θαυμάσῃς: aor. subj. in prohibition, "don't marvel!"

ΜΕΝΕΛΑΟΣ: Εἶδον καὶ αὐτός· ἀλλά μοι δοκεῖς — εἰρήσεται γὰρ πρὸς σέ — γοητείαν τινὰ προσάγειν τῷ πράγματι καὶ τοὺς ὀφθαλμοὺς ἐξαπατᾶν τῶν ὁρώντων αὐτὸς οὐδὲν τοιοῦτο γιγνόμενος.

γοητεία, ἡ: finesse
ἐξαπατάω: to deceive or beguile thoroughly
ὁράω: to see

προσάγω: to introduce X (*acc.*) into Y (*dat.*)
τοιοῦτος, -αύτη, -οῦτο: such as this

εἰρήσεται: fut. perf. of λέγω, "for *it will be said* to you"
προσάγειν ... ἐξαπατᾶν: pr. infs. after δοκεῖς, "you seem *to introduce ... to deceive*"
τῶν ὁρώντων: pr. part., "of the onlookers."
γιγνόμενος: pr. part., "you yourself *becoming*"

οἶδα and εἶδον

Observe the irregular present of **οἶδα**:

οἶδα	I know	ἴσμεν	we know
οἶσθα	you know	ἴστε	you know
οἶδε	she knows	ἴσασι	they know

These forms are actually from the perfect system of the aorist verb stem Ϝιδ- (where Ϝ is the lost letter digamma that sounds like a "w," cf. Latin vid-) meaning "to see," and **οἶδα** means "I have seen" and therefore "I know." The future is **εἴσομαι**.

The same verb stem also forms the strong aorist **εἶδον** (from ἐ-Ϝ-ιδον), "I saw." From the unaugmented form of this verb we have the imperative (ἴδε, ἰδού), the participle (ἰδών, ἰδοῦσα) the subjunctive (ἴδω, ἴδῃς, ἴδῃ) and the optative (ἴδοι).

For the present, the verb **ὁράω** is used. This verb also has a perfect, **ἑώρακα**, which emphasizes the act of seeing itself. Note the perfect infinitive, **ἑωρακέναι**. Note also the imperfect of **ὁράω**:

ἑώρων	I was seeing
ἑώρας	you were seeing
ἑώρα	he was seeing

Yet another stem (-οπ) is used for the future, the perfect, and the aorist passive. Here is a synopsis of these verbs:

Present	Future	Aorist	Perfect	Aorist Passive
ὁράω			ἑώρακα	
		εἶδον	οἶδα	
	ὄψομαι		ὄπωπα	ὤφθην

ΠΡΩΤΕΥΣ: Καὶ τίς ἂν ἡ ἀπάτη ἐπὶ τῶν οὕτως ἐναργῶν γένοιτο; οὐκ ἀνεῳγμένοις τοῖς ὀφθαλμοῖς εἶδες, εἰς ὅσα μετεποίησα ἐμαυτόν; εἰ δὲ ἀπιστεῖς καὶ τὸ πρᾶγμα ψευδὲς εἶναι δοκεῖ, καὶ φαντασία τις πρὸ τῶν ὀφθαλμῶν ἱσταμένη, ἐπειδὰν πῦρ γένωμαι, προσένεγκέ μοι, ὦ γενναιότατε, τὴν χεῖρα· εἴσῃ γάρ, εἰ ὁρῶμαι μόνον ἢ καὶ τὸ κάειν τότε μοι πρόσεστιν.

ἀνοίγνυμι: to open
ἀπάτη, ἡ: a trick, fraud, deceit
ἀπιστέω: to disbelieve
γενναῖος, -α, -ον: noble
ἐναργής, -ές: visible
ἐπειδάν: whenever
ἵστημι: to make to stand
καίω: to burn
μεταποιέω: to alter
μόνος, -η, -ον: alone

οἶδα: to know
ὅσος, -η, -ον: what sort of
πρᾶγμα, -ατος, τό: a deed, matter
πρόσειμι: to be possible
προσφέρω: to bring to
πῦρ, τό: fire
φαντασία, ἡ: an illusion
χείρ, χειρός, ἡ: a hand
ψευδής, -ές: lying, false

ἂν γένοιτο: aor. opt. pot., "what deception *could there be?*"
οὐκ ... εἶδες: aor., "did you not see?" with the expectation of a positive answer
ἀνεῳγμένοις: perf. part., "with eyes *opened*"
ἱσταμένη: pr. part., "being set up"
ἐπειδὰν γένωμαι: aor. subj. in pr. gen. temp. cl., "whenever I become fire"
προσένεγκέ: aor. imper. of προσφέρω, "present!"
εἴσῃ: fut. of οἶδα, "you will know"
εἰ ὁρῶμαι: pr. pass. in ind. quest. after εἴσῃ, "know *whether I am being seen* only"
τὸ κάειν: articlular inf., subject of πρόσεστιν, "whether *the burning* is possible"

Other General or Indefinite Clauses

A general or indefinite temporal clause in the present has the same form as a present general condition (see p. 6), with ἐπειδὰν (whenever) or ὅταν instead of ἐὰν with the subjunctive.

ἐπειδὰν πῦρ γένωμαι, προσένεγκέ μοι, ὦ γενναῖε, τὴν χεῖρα: "whenever I become fire, give me, o noble one, your hand"

Compare also with general relative clauses:

ὁποίᾳ ἂν πέτρᾳ ἁρμόσῃ τὰς κοτύλας ... ἐκείνῃ ὅμοιον ἐργάζεται ἑαυτὸν: to whatever rock he attaches his suckers ... to that rock he makes himself similar.

Dialogues of the Sea Gods

ΜΕΝΕΛΑΟΣ: Οὐκ ἀσφαλὴς ἡ πεῖρα, ὦ Πρωτεῦ.

ΠΡΩΤΕΥΣ: Σὺ δέ μοι, Μενέλαε, δοκεῖς οὐδὲ πολύπουν ἑωρακέναι πώποτε οὐδὲ ὃ πάσχει ὁ ἰχθῦς οὗτος εἰδέναι.

ΜΕΝΕΛΑΟΣ: Ἀλλὰ τὸν μὲν πολύπουν εἶδον, ἃ πάσχει δέ, ἡδέως ἂν μάθοιμι παρὰ σοῦ.

ἀσφαλής, -ές: steadfast, firm
ἡδέως: gladly
ἰχθῦς, ὁ: a fish
μανθάνω: to learn
οἶδα: to know

πάσχω: to experience
πεῖρα, ἡ: a trial, attempt, essay, experiment
πολύπους, ὁ: an octopus
πώποτε: ever yet

ἑωρακέναι: perf. infin. of ὁράω complementing δοκεῖς, "you do not seem *to have seen.*"
εἰδέναι: perf. infin. also complementing δοκεῖς, "nor do you seem *to know*"
ἂν μάθοιμι: aor. opt. pot., "I would like to learn"
παρὰ σοῦ: "from you."

Note the different meanings of the word αὐτός

1. The nominative forms of the word without the definite article are always intensive (= Latin ipse): αὐτὸς: "*he himself*," αὐτοί, "*they themselves.*"
   αὐτὸς οὐδὲν τοιοῦτο γιγνόμενος, "*you yourself* becoming nothing else."
   καὶ τὸ σπήλαιον αὐτὸ ἀνεστρέφετο, "and the cave *itself* was spinning"
   The other cases of the word are also intensive when they modify a noun or pronoun, either without the definite article or in predicative position:
   αὐτὸν δὲ ἐμὲ ὑπερκαχλάσαι ποιήσας, "causing *me myself* to bubble over"
2. Oblique cases of the word, when used without a noun or a definite article, are the unemphatic third person pronouns: him, them, etc.:
   αὐτὴν εἰς Αἴγυπτον ἔπεμψεν, "he sent *her* to Egypt."
   This is the most common use in the *Dialogues of the Sea Gods*.
3. Any case of the word with an article in attributive position means "the same":
   τὰ αὐτὰ καὶ ἡ Ἰνὼ πείσεται, "Ino will suffer *the same things.*"

ΠΡΩΤΕΥΣ: Ὁποίᾳ ἂν πέτρᾳ προσελθὼν ἁρμόσῃ τὰς κοτύλας καὶ προσφὺς ἔχηται κατὰ τὰς πλεκτάνας, ἐκείνῃ ὅμοιον ἀπεργάζεται ἑαυτὸν καὶ μεταβάλλει τὴν χρόαν μιμούμενος τὴν πέτραν, ὡς λανθάνειν τοὺς ἁλιέας μὴ διαλλάττων μηδὲ φανερὸς ὢν διὰ τοῦτο, ἀλλὰ ἐοικὼς τῷ λίθῳ.

ἁλιεύς, ὁ: a fisherman
ἀπεργάζομαι: to affect, make
ἁρμόζω: to fit together, join
διαλλάττω: to change, to become different
ἔοικα: be similar to (+ dat.)
κοτύλη, ἡ: a sucker
λανθάνω: to escape notice
λίθος, ὁ: a stone
μεταβάλλω: to turn quickly, change

μιμέομαι: to mimic, imitate
ὅμοιος, -α, -ον: like, resembling
πέτρα, ἡ: a rock, a ledge or shelf of rock
πλεκτάνη, ἡ: a coil, tentacle
προσέρχομαι: to come or go to
προσφύω: to cling to
φανερός, -όν: conspicuous
χρόα, ἡ: the surface of a body, skin

ὁποίᾳ ἂν ... ἁρμόσῃ: aor. subj. in gen. rel. cl., "*to whatever* rock it *attaches* its suckers"
προσελθών: aor. part., "having approached"
προσφύς: aor. part., "having clung fast to"
ἔχηται: pr. subj. mid. also in pr. gen. rel. cl., "to whatever rock *it fastens itself*"
ὅμοιον: acc. pred., "makes himself *similar to*" + dat.
ὡς λανθάνειν: pr. inf. in res. cl., "so that he escapes the notice"
μὴ διαλλάττων: pr. part. instrumental, "by not being different to"
μηδὲ φανερὸς ὤν: pr. part. instrumental, "by not being conspicuous"
ἐοικώς: perf. part., "but *by being similar to*" + dat.

Result Clauses

ὥστε (sometimes ὡς) introduces result clauses either with an infinitive or with a finite verb.

ὥστε + infinitive indicates a possible or intended result, without emphasizing its actual occurrence. The infinitive does not express time, but only aspect.

ὥστε + indicative emphasizes the actual occurence of the result. Both time and aspect are indicated by the form of the verb.

μεταβάλλει τὴν χροίαν μιμούμενος τὴν πέτραν, ὡς λανθάνειν τοὺς ἁλιέας: "he changes his color by imitating the rock so that (in order that) he escapes the notice of fishermen."

ἀπάξει αὐτὴν εἰς Ἄργος, ὥστε ἀντὶ θανάτου γάμον οὐ τὸν τυχόντα εὕρετο. "He will lead her to Argos, and so she has found an unusual marriage instead of death."

ΜΕΝΕΛΑΟΣ: Φασὶ ταῦτα: τὸ δὲ σὸν πολλῷ παραδοξότερον, ὦ Πρωτεῦ.

ΠΡΩΤΕΥΣ: Οὐκ οἶδα, ὦ Μενέλαε, τίνι ἂν ἄλλῳ πιστεύσειας τοῖς σεαυτοῦ ὀφθαλμοῖς ἀπιστῶν.

ΜΕΝΕΛΑΟΣ: Εἶδον: ἀλλὰ τὸ πρᾶγμα τεράστιον, ὁ αὐτὸς πῦρ καὶ ὕδωρ.

Proteus from Andrea Alciato, Emblemata, *1531.*

ἀπιστέω: to disbelieve (+ *dat.*)
λίθος, ὁ: a stone
ὀφθαλμός, ὁ: an eye
παράδοξος, -ον: paradoxical
πιστεύω: to trust, believe in (+ *dat.*)

πρᾶγμα, -ατος, τό: a deed, act, matter
πῦρ, τό: fire
τεράστιος, -ον: monstrous
ὕδωρ, -ατος, τό: water
φημί: to declare, make known

παραδοξότερον: nom. pred., "your case is *more paradoxical*"
τίνι ἂν ἄλλῳ πιστεύσειας: aor. opt. pot. in rel. cl., "in what other thing you might believe"
πῦρ καὶ ὕδωρ: nom. pred., "the same person is *fire and water*"

5 (7). Panope and Galene

In this dialogue a sea nymph, "All-seeing," recounts to another, "Calm," what she witnessed at the marriage of Peleus and Thetis. The uninvited Eris causes a competition among the goddesses leading to the judgement of Paris. The judgement itself has not yet been concluded, but Galene predicts that Aphrodite will be the winner.

ΠΑΝΟΠΗ: Εἶδες, ὦ Γαλήνη, χθὲς οἷα ἐποίησεν ἡ Ἔρις παρὰ τὸ δεῖπνον ἐν Θετταλίᾳ, διότι μὴ καὶ αὐτὴ ἐκλήθη εἰς τὸ συμπόσιον;

ΓΑΛΗΝΗ: Οὐ ξυνειστιώμην ὑμῖν ἔγωγε· ὁ γὰρ Ποσειδῶν ἐκέλευσέ με, ὦ Πανόπη, ἀκύμαντον ἐν τοσούτῳ φυλάττειν τὸ πέλαγος. τί δ' οὖν ἐποίησεν ἡ Ἔρις μὴ παροῦσα;

ἀκύμαντος, -ον: not washed by the waves, calm
Γαλήνη, ἡ: Galene, a Nereid, "calm"
δεῖπνον, τό: the principal meal
διότι: for the reason that, since
εἶδον: to see
Ἔρις, ἡ: Eris
Θετταλία, ἡ: Thessaly
καλέω: to call, summon, invite

κελεύω: to order, urge, exhort
ξυνεστιάω: to feast together
Πανόπη, ἡ: Panope, a Nereid, "all seeing"
πάρειμι: to be present
πέλαγος, -ους, τό: the sea
ποιέω: to make, to do
συμπόσιον, τό: a drinking-party, symposium
φυλάττω: to keep guard
χθές: yesterday

Ἔρις: Eris was the goddess of discord
διότι μὴ ... ἐκλήθη: aor. pass. of καλέω, "because she was not invited"
ξυνειστιώμην: impf., "I was not feasting with you"
ἐν τοσούτῳ (sc. χρόνῳ): "in the meantime"
φυλάττειν: pr. inf. after ἐκέλευσέ, "ordered me *to keep*"
μὴ παροῦσα: pr. part. conditional, "if not being present"

Dialogues of the Sea Gods

ΠΑΝΟΠΗ: Ἡ Θέτις μὲν ἤδη καὶ ὁ Πηλεὺς ἀπεληλύθεσαν ἐς τὸν θάλαμον ὑπὸ τῆς Ἀμφιτρίτης καὶ τοῦ Ποσειδῶνος παραπεμφθέντες, ἡ Ἔρις δὲ ἐν τοσούτῳ λαθοῦσα πάντας — ἐδυνήθη δὲ ῥᾳδίως, τῶν μὲν πινόντων,

---

Ἀμφιτρίτη, ἡ: Amphitrite
ἀπέρχομαι: to go away, depart from
δύναμαι: to be able
θάλαμος, ὁ: an inner room or chamber
Θέτις, Θέτιδος, ἡ: Thetis

λανθάνω: to escape notice, to be unnoticed
παραπέμπω: to send past, convey
Πηλεύς, -έως, ὁ: Peleus
πίνω: to drink
ῥᾴδιος, -α, -ον: easy, ready

ἀπεληλύθεσαν: plupf., "Thetis and Peleus *had departed*"
παραπεμφθέντες: aor. part. pass., "having been escorted"
ἐν τοσούτῳ (sc. χρόνῳ): "in the meantime"
λαθοῦσα: aor. part. supplementing ἐδυνήθη, "she was able *to escape the notice of* all"
τῶν μὲν πινόντων: pr. part. in gen. abs., "some were drinking"

Circumstantial Participles

Circumstantial participles are added to a noun or a pronoun to set forth some circumstance under which an action takes place. The circumstances can be of the following types: time, manner, means, cause, purpose, concession, condition or attendant circumstance. Although sometimes particles can specify the type of circumstance, often only the context can clarify its force. Here are some examples:

Time: ἀποκρίνεσθαι αὐτῷ ἤθελεν ... βρυχομένῳ: "she would not wish to answer him *when he is gnashing* his teeth"

Means: οὔτε ἀναπαύεις σεαυτὸν διαχυθείς: "nor do you rest *by dispersing* yourself."

Purpose: ἔπεσεν εἰς τὴν θάλατταν ὡς αὐτίκα πάντως ἀποθανούμενος: "he fell into the sea *in order to die* immediately." ὡς is often used in these cases to indicate an alleged purpose.

Concession: ἀποκρίνεσθαι αὐτῷ ἤθελεν οὕτω λάλος οὖσα: "she would not wish to answer him, *although being* talkative"

Cause: ἀλλὰ ὕδωρ μέν σε γενέσθαι, ὦ Πρωτεῦ, οὐκ ἀπίθανον, ἐνάλιόν γε ὄντα: "It is not unpersuasive that you become water, Proteus, *since you are* of the sea."

Condition: τί δ' οὖν ἐποίησεν ἡ Ἔρις μὴ παροῦσα; "What then did Eris do, *if she was not present.*" Note that μή is used instead of οὐ when the participle is conditional.

Attendant circumstance: οὐκ ἐχρῆν οὕτω πονηρὰν οὖσαν: "It was not necessary for (a woman) *who was* so bad"

οὐκ ἄλλη κρατήσει τῆς Ἀφροδίτης ἀγωνιζομένης: "no other will win *with Aphrodite contending.*"

Note that the last example is a *genitive absolute*, of which there are a large number in the *Dialogi Marini*.

ἐνίων δὲ κροτούντων ἢ τῷ Ἀπόλλωνι κιθαρίζοντι ἢ ταῖς Μούσαις ᾀδούσαις προσεχόντων τὸν νοῦν — ἐνέβαλεν ἐς τὸ ξυμπόσιον μῆλόν τι πάγκαλον, χρυσοῦν ὅλον, ὦ Γαλήνη· ἐπεγέγραπτο δὲ «ἡ καλὴ λαβέτω.» κυλινδούμενον δὲ τοῦτο ὥσπερ ἐξεπίτηδες ἧκεν ἔνθα Ἥρα τε καὶ Ἀφροδίτη καὶ Ἀθηνᾶ κατεκλίνοντο. κἀπειδὴ ὁ Ἑρμῆς ἀνελόμενος ἐπελέξατο τὰ γεγραμμένα, αἱ μὲν Νηρεΐδες ἡμεῖς ἀπεσιωπήσαμεν. τί γὰρ ἔδει ποιεῖν ἐκείνων παρουσῶν; αἱ δὲ ἀντεποιοῦντο ἑκάστη καὶ αὐτῆς

ᾄδω: to sing
Ἀθηνᾶ, ἡ: Athena
ἀναιρέω: to take up, raise
ἀντιποιέω: to contend for
Ἀπόλλων, -ωνος, ὁ: Apollo
ἀποσιωπάω: to be silent
Ἀφροδίτη, ἡ: Aphrodite
γράφω: to scratch, scrape, graze
δεῖ: it is necessary
ἐμβάλλω: to throw in
ἐξεπίτηδες: (adv.) of set purpose
ἐπιγράφω: to mark the surface, inscribe
ἐπιλέγομαι: to choose, read
Ἑρμῆς, -οῦ, ὁ: Hermes
ἥκω: to have come, be present, be here
Ἥρα, ἡ: Hera

καλός, -ή, -όν: beautiful
κατακλίνω: to lay down
κιθαρίζω: to play the cithara
κροτέω: to rattle, to applaud
κυλινδέω: to roll
μῆλον, τό: apple
Μοῦσα, -ης, ἡ: a Muse
Νηρηΐς, -ΐδος, ἡ: a daughter of Nereus, a Nereid
νοῦς, ὁ: mind, attention
ὅλος, -η, -ον: whole, entire
πάγκαλος, -η, -ον: all beautiful
πάρειμι: to be present
προσέχω: to hold to, offer
χρύσεος, -η, -ον: golden, of gold

ἐνίων δὲ κροτούντων: pr. part. in gen. abs., "and others were applauding"
προσεχόντων: pr. part., "while *offering* their attention to" + dat.
ἐνέβαλεν: aor., "she threw in"
ἐπεγέγραπτο: plup. pass., "on it *had been inscribed*."
λαβέτω: aor. imper. 3 s., "let her take it!"
ἔνθα ... κατεκλίνοντο: impf. of κατα-κλίνω, "where they were lying down"
κἀπειδὴ: (=καί ἐπειδή), "and after"
ἀνελόμενος: aor. part., "having taken up"
ἐπελέξατο: aor., "he read outloud"
τὰ γεγραμμένα: perf. part., "the inscriptions"
ἀπεσιωπήσαμεν: aor., "we Nereids *were silent*"
ἐκείνων παρουσῶν: gen. abs., "with them being present"
αἱ δὲ: "but they," i.e. the three goddesses
αὐτῆς: gen. complement, "the apple to be *hers*"

εἶναι τὸ μῆλον ἠξίουν, καὶ εἰ μή γε ὁ Ζεὺς διέστησεν αὐτάς, καὶ ἄχρι χειρῶν ἂν τὸ πρᾶγμα προὐχώρησεν. ἀλλ' ἐκεῖνος, «Αὐτὸς μὲν οὐ κρινῶ» φησί, «περὶ τούτου,» καίτοι ἐκεῖναι αὐτὸν δικάσαι ἠξίουν, «ἄπιτε δὲ ἐς τὴν Ἴδην παρὰ τὸν Πριάμου παῖδα, ὃς οἶδέ τε διαγνῶναι τὸ κάλλιον φιλόκαλος ὤν, καὶ οὐκ ἂν ἐκεῖνος κρίναι κακῶς.»

ἀξιόω: to think worthy to, to ask (+ *inf.*)
ἄχρι: all the way up to (+ *gen.*)
διαγιγνώσκω: to distinguish, discern
διΐστημι: to set apart, separate
δικάζω: to judge, to give judgment on
Ζεύς, ὁ: Zeus
Ἴδη, ἡ: Mt. Ida, near Troy
καλλίων, κάλλιον: more beautiful
κρίνω: to pick out, choose

μῆλον, τό: apple
οἶδα: to know
παῖς, παιδός, ὁ: a child
πρᾶγμα, -ατος, τό: a deed, matter
Πρίαμος, ὁ: Priam, father of Paris
προχωρέω: to go or come forward, advance
φιλόκαλος, -ον: loving the beautiful
χείρ, χειρός, ἡ: a hand

εἰ μή ... διέστησεν: aor. of δια-ἵστημι in past contrafactual protasis, "if Zeus had not separated them"
ἄχρι χειρῶν: "to hands" i.e. to blows
ἂν ... προὐχώρησεν: aor. of προ-χωρέω in past contrafactual apodosis, "the matter would have progressed"
οὐ κρινῶ: fut., "I will not choose"
καίτοι ... ἠξίουν: impf. concessive, "although those were asking him" + inf.
ἄπιτε: pr. imper., "go!"
διαγνῶναι: aor. inf. after οἶδέ, "he knows how *to discern*"
ὤν: pr. part. causal, "since he is"
ἂν ... κρίναι: aor. opt. pot., "he would not choose."

More conditions

The future more vivid condition indicates a probability, rather than a possibility. It has ἐάν (Attic contraction = ἤν) plus subjunctive in the protasis, future indicative in the apodosis: translate "if he does... then he will...."

οὐκ ἄλλη κρατήσει ... ἢν μὴ ἀμβλυώττῃ: "another will not win, unless the judge is dim-sighted"

A past contrafactual condition has εἰ plus the aorist indicative in the protasis, ἂν plus the aorist indicative in the apodosis: translate "if he had done ... then he would have" (but he didn't).

καὶ εἰ μή γε ὁ Ζεὺς διέστησεν αὐτάς, καὶ ἄχρι χειρῶν ἂν τὸ πρᾶγμα προὐχώρησεν: "If Zeus had not separated them, the matter would have come to blows (but it didn't)."

ΓΑΛΗΝΗ: Τί οὖν αἱ θεαί, ὦ Πανόπη;

ΠΑΝΟΠΗ: Τήμερον, οἶμαι, ἀπίασιν εἰς τὴν Ἴδην, καί τις ἥξει μετὰ μικρὸν ἀπαγγέλλων ἡμῖν τὴν κρατοῦσαν.

ΓΑΛΗΝΗ: Ἤδη σοί φημι, οὐκ ἄλλη κρατήσει τῆς Ἀφροδίτης ἀγωνιζομένης, ἢν μὴ πάνυ ὁ διαιτητὴς ἀμβλυώττῃ.

Peleus greeting wedding procession leading Thetis to his house, **black figure** dinos *of Sophilos (c. 580 BCE)*

ἀγωνίζομαι: to contend for a prize	ἥκω: to have come, be present, be here
ἀμβλυώττω: to be dim-sighted	θεά, ἡ: a goddess
ἀπαγγέλλω: to bring tidings, report, announce	κρατέω: to be strong, to conquer
	μικρός, -ά, -όν: small, little
ἀπέρχομαι: to go away	οἶμαι: to suppose, think
διαιτητής, -οῦ, ὁ: an arbitrator, umpire	τήμερον: today

ἀπίασιν: fut., "they will go"

μετὰ μικρὸν (sc. χρόνον): "shortly."

ἀπαγγέλλων: pr. part. suppl. ἥξει, "someone will come *announcing*"

τὴν κρατοῦσαν: pr. part., "the one winning"

τῆς Ἀφροδίτης ἀγωνιζομένης: pr. part. in gen. abs., "with Aphrodite contending for a prize"

ἢν μὴ ... ἀμβλυώττῃ: pr. subj. in fut. more vivid protasis, "unless the judge is dim-sighted"

6 (8). Triton, Poseidon and Amyone

Amyone is one of the fifty daughters of Danaus, who were married to the fifty daughters of Aegyptus. On their wedding night, all but one kills her husband, for which they are punished in the underworld by the perpetual task of carrying water. Part of this story is told in Aeschylus' Suppliants, and the story of Amyone was treated in the (now lost) satyr play that accompanied the performance of the Suppliants. In other versions Poseidon saves Amyone from a satyr, but regularly resolves to provide a fountain in exchange for her favors.

ΤΡΙΤΩΝ: Ἐπὶ τὴν Λέρναν, ὦ Πόσειδον, παραγίνεται καθ' ἑκάστην ἡμέραν ὑδρευσομένη παρθένος, πάγκαλόν τι χρῆμα: οὐκ οἶδα ἔγωγε καλλίω παῖδα ἰδών.

ΠΟΣΕΙΔΩΝ: Ἐλευθέραν τινά, ὦ Τρίτων, λέγεις, ἢ θεράπαινά τις ὑδροφόρος ἐστίν;

ΤΡΙΤΩΝ: Οὐ μὲν οὖν, ἀλλὰ τοῦ Αἰγυπτίου ἐκείνου θυγάτηρ, μία τῶν πεντήκοντα καὶ αὐτή, Ἀμυμώνη τοὔνομα:

Αἰγύπτιος, -α, -ον: Egyptian
Ἀμυμώνη, ἡ: Amymone, daughter of Danaus
ἕκαστος, -η, -ον: every, every one, each
ἐλεύθερος, -α, -ον: free
ἡμέρα, ἡ: a day
θεράπαινα, ἡ: a waiting maid, handmaid
θυγάτηρ, -έρος, ἡ: a daughter
καλλίων, κάλλιον: more beautiful
Λέρνα, ἡ: Lerna, a region south of Argos
οἶδα: to know
ὄνομα, τό: a name

πάγκαλός, -η, -ον: completely beautiful
παῖς, παιδός, ἡ: a child
παραγίνομαι: appears, approaches
παρθένος, -ου, ἡ: a maid
πεντήκοντα, -indecl. οἱ: fifty
Ποσειδῶν, -ῶνος, ὁ: Poseidon
Τρίτων, -ωνος, ὁ: Triton
ὑδρεύω: to draw, fetch or carry water
ὑδροφόρος, -η, -ον: carrying water
χρῆμα, τό: a creature

ὑδρευσομένη: fut. part. indicating purpose, "in order to draw water"
ἰδών: aor. part. in ind. st., "I don't know *that I saw* a prettier girl."
καλλίω: acc. s. (=καλλίο(ν)α), "prettier"
οὐ μὲν οὖν: "no, not at all"
Ἀμυμώνη: Amymone, the "blameless one," was a daughter of Danaus.
τοὔνομα: (=τό ὄνομα), acc. of respect, "by name"

ἐπυθόμην γὰρ ἥτις καλοῖτο καὶ τὸ γένος. ὁ Δαναὸς δὲ σκληραγωγεῖ τὰς θυγατέρας καὶ αὐτουργεῖν διδάσκει καὶ πέμπει ὕδωρ τε ἀρυσομένας καὶ πρὸς τὰ ἄλλα παιδεύει ἀόκνους εἶναι αὐτάς.

ΠΟΣΕΙΔΩΝ: Μόνη δὲ παραγίνεται μακρὰν οὕτω τὴν ὁδὸν ἐξ Ἄργους εἰς Λέρναν;

ΤΡΙΤΩΝ: Μόνη· πολυδίψιον δὲ τὸ Ἄργος, ὡς οἶσθα· ὥστε ἀνάγκη ἀεὶ ὑδροφορεῖν.

ΠΟΣΕΙΔΩΝ: Ὦ Τρίτων, οὐ μετρίως διετάραξας με εἰπὼν τὰ περὶ τῆς παιδός· ὥστε ἴωμεν ἐπ' αὐτήν.

ἀνάγκη, ἡ: necessity
ἄοκνος, -ον: without hesitation, untiring
Ἄργος, Ἄργους, ὁ: Argos
ἀρύω: to draw
αὐτουργέω: to work with one's own hand
γένος, -ους, τό: a race, stock, family
Δαναὸς, ὁ: Danaus
διαταράττω: to throw into great confusion
διδάσκω: to teach, instruct
θυγάτηρ, -έρος, ἡ: a daughter
καλέω: to call
μακρός, -ά, -όν: long
μέτριος, -α, -ον: within measure

μόνος, -η, -ον: alone, left alone
ὁδός, ἡ: a way, path, track, road
παιδεύω: to bring up or rear a child
παραγίνομαι: appears, approach
πέμπω: to send
πολυδίψιος, -ον: very thirsty
πυνθάνομαι: to learn by hearsay or by inquiry
σκληραγωγέω: to bring up hardy
Τρίτων, -ωνος, ὁ: Triton
ὑδροφορέω: to carry water
ὕδωρ, -ατος, τό: water

καλοῖτο: pr. opt. in ind. quest., "I learned *what she is called*"
αὐτουργεῖν: pr. inf. after **διδάσκει**, "teaches them *to work with their own hands*"
ἀρυσομένας: fut. mid. part. of **ἀρύω** expressing purpose, "he sends them *in order to fetch*"
ἀόκνους: acc. pred., "teaches them *to be untiring*"
μακρὰν οὕτω τὴν ὁδόν: acc. of duration, "*such a long journey*"
ὥστε ἀνάγκη (sc. ἐστι): res. cl., "*so that it is necessary* to carry water"
διετάραξας: aor. of **δια-ταράττω**, "*you have confounded*"
εἰπὼν: aor. part. instrumental, "*by speaking* about the girl"
ὥστε ἴωμεν: pres. subj. jussive, "*and so let us go*"

ΤΡΙΤΩΝ: Ἴωμεν: ἤδη γοῦν καιρὸς τῆς ὑδροφορίας: καὶ σχεδόν που κατὰ μέσην τὴν ὁδόν ἐστιν ἰοῦσα ἐς τὴν Λέρναν.

ΠΟΣΕΙΔΩΝ: Οὐκοῦν ζεῦξον τὸ ἅρμα: ἢ τοῦτο μὲν πολλὴν ἔχει τὴν διατριβὴν ὑπάγειν τοὺς ἵππους τῇ ζεύγλῃ καὶ τὸ ἅρμα ἐπισκευάζειν, σὺ δὲ ἀλλὰ δελφῖνά μοί τινα τῶν ὠκέων παράστησον: ἀφιππάσομαι γὰρ ἐπ' αὐτοῦ τάχιστα.

ΤΡΙΤΩΝ: Ἰδού σοι οὑτοσὶ δελφίνων ὁ ὠκύτατος.

ΠΟΣΕΙΔΩΝ: Εὖ γε: ἀπελαύνωμεν: σὺ δὲ παρανήχου, ὦ Τρίτων. κἀπειδὴ πάρεσμεν εἰς τὴν Λέρναν, ἐγὼ μὲν

ἀπελαύνω: to drive away, to drive off
ἅρμα, -ατος, τό: a chariot
ἀφιππάζομαι: to ride off or away
δελφίς, -ῖνος, ὁ: a dolphin
διατριβή, ἡ: a way of spending time
ἐπισκευάζω: to get ready, to equip, fit out
ζεύγλη, ἡ: a strap or loop of the yoke
ζεύγνυμι: to yoke, put to
ἵππος, ὁ: a horse, mare
καιρός, ὁ: due measure, proper time
μέσος, -η, -ον: middle, in the middle

οὐκοῦν: therefore, then, accordingly
παρανήχομαι: to swim along
πάρειμι: to be present
παρίστημι: to make to stand or to place beside
σχεδόν: close, near, hard by, nigh
ταχύς, -εῖα, -ύ: quick, swift, fleet
ὑδροφορία, ἡ: a water-carrying
ὑπάγω: to lead X (acc.) under Y (dat.)
ὠκύς, εῖα, -ύ: quick, swift, fleet

ἰοῦσα: pr. part. of εἶμι, "she *going*"
ζεῦξον: aor. imper., "harness!"
ἢ τοῦτο μὲν ... σὺ δὲ: "or rather this ... so instead you"
πολλὴν ἔχει τὴν διατριβὴν: acc. of duration, "this *takes too much time*"
ὑπάγειν: pr. inf. expressing purpose after διατριβὴν, "time *to lead under*"
ἐπισκευάζειν: pr. inf. also after διατριβὴν, "time *to get ready*"
παράστησον: aor. imper. of παρα-ἵστημι, "fetch!"
ἀφιππάσομαι: fut., "I will ride off"
Ἰδού: aor. imper. from εἶδον, "look!"
οὑτοσὶ: nom. s. with deictic particle -ι, "this one here"
ἀπελαύνωμεν: pres. subj. jussive, "let us depart"

λοχήσω ἐνταῦθά που, σὺ δὲ ἀποσκόπει: ὁπόταν αἴσθῃ προσιοῦσαν αὐτὴν —

ΤΡΙΤΩΝ: Αὕτη σοι πλησίον.

ΠΟΣΕΙΔΩΝ: Καλή, ὦ Τρίτων, καὶ ὡραία παρθένος: ἀλλὰ συλληπτέα ἡμῖν ἐστιν.

ΑΜΥΜΩΝΗ: Ἄνθρωπε, ποῖ με συναρπάσας ἄγεις; ἀνδραποδιστὴς εἶ, καὶ ἔοικας ἡμῖν ὑπ' Αἰγύπτου τοῦ θείου ἐπιπεμφθῆναι: ὥστε βοήσομαι τὸν πατέρα.

ΤΡΙΤΩΝ: Σιώπησον, ὦ Ἀμυμώνη: Ποσειδῶν ἐστι.

ἄγω: to lead or carry, to convey, bring
Αἴγυπτος, ὁ: Aegyptus
αἰσθάνομαι: to perceive, to see
ἀνδραποδιστής, ὁ: a kidnapper
ἀποσκοπέω: to look out, keep watch
βοάω: to cry aloud, to shout
ἔοικα: to seem to (+ *inf.*)
ἐπιπέμπω: to send against
θεῖος, ὁ: an uncle
λοχάω: to lie in wait for, to watch, entrap

ὁπόταν: whensoever (+ *subj.*)
παρθένος, -ου, ἡ: a maid, maiden
πατήρ, πατρός, ὁ: a father
πλησίον: nearby to (+ *dat.*)
προσέρχομαι: to approach
σιωπάω: to be silent
συλλαμβάνω: to seize
συναρπάζω: to seize and carry away
ὡραῖος, -α, -ον: blooming, ripe

λοχήσω: fut., "I will lie in wait"
ἀποσκόπει: pr. imper., "keep watch!"
ὁπόταν αἴσθῃ: aor. subj. in gen. temp. cls., "whenever you perceive"
προσιοῦσαν: pr. part., "perceive *her approaching*"
συλληπτέα ἐστιν: verbal adj. of **συλλαμβάνω** in periphrastic, "she must be seized"
ἡμῖν: dat. of agent, "by us"
συναρπάσας: aor. part., "you, *having seized* me"
ἐπιπεμφθῆναι: aor. pass. inf. of **ἐπι-πέμπω**, complementing **ἔοικας**, "seem *to have been sent against*"
ὑπ' Αἰγύπτου: Aegyptus's fifty sons came to Argos to capture their reluctant brides.
ὥστε βοήσομαι: fut. in res. cl., "and so I will call out"
σιώπησον: aor. imper., "be silent!"

ΑΜΥΜΩΝΗ: Τί Ποσειδῶν λέγεις; τί βιάζῃ με, ὦ ἄνθρωπε, καὶ εἰς τὴν θάλατταν καθέλκεις; ἐγὼ δὲ ἀποπνιγήσομαι ἡ ἀθλία καταδῦσα.

ΠΟΣΕΙΔΩΝ: Θάρρει, οὐδὲν δεινὸν μὴ πάθῃς· ἀλλὰ καὶ πηγὴν ἐπώνυμον σοι ἀναδοθῆναί ἐάσω ἐνταῦθα πατάξας τῇ τριαίνῃ τὴν πέτραν πλησίον τοῦ κλύσματος, καὶ σὺ εὐδαίμων ἔσῃ καὶ μόνη τῶν ἀδελφῶν οὐχ ὑδροφορήσεις ἀποθανοῦσα.

ἀδελφή, ἡ: a sister
ἄθλιος, -α, -ον: miserable
ἀναδίδωμι: to give forth or up
ἀποθνῄσκω: to die
ἀποπνίγω: to choke
βιάζω: to constrain
δεινός, -ή, -όν: fearful, terrible
ἐάω: to allow + inf.
ἐπώνυμος, -ον: given as a name, eponymous
εὐδαίμων, -ον: blessed
θάλαττα, ἡ: the sea
θαρρέω: to be of good courage, take courage

καθέλκω: to draw
καταδύω: to go down, sink, set
κλύσμα, -ατος, τό: a washing place, beach
λέγω: to say, mean
μόνος, -η, -ον: alone, only
πάσχω: to suffer, experience
πατάττω: to beat, knock, strike
πέτρα, ἡ: a rock, a ledge or shelf of rock
πηγή, ἡ: running water, stream
πλησίον: next to (+ *gen.*)
τρίαινα, ἡ: a trident
ὑδροφορέω: to carry water

τί βιάζῃ: pr. mid., "*why do you restrain me?*"
καταδῦσα: aor. part., "I, *having submerged*"
θάρρει: pr. imper., "be of good courage!"
μὴ πάθῃς: aor. subj. in clause of fearing after **θάρρει**, "have courage that you will not suffer!"
ἀλλὰ καί: "on the contrary"
ἀναδοθῆναί: aor. pass. inf. after **ἐάσω**, "I will allow a stream *to burst forth*"
σοι: dat. of advant., "for you"
πατάξας: aor. part. instrumental, "by striking"
ἔσῃ: fut. mid. of **εἰμί**, "you will be"
οὐχ ὑδροφορήσεις: "you will not carry waters," a reference to the punishment of the Danaids who killed their husbands.
ἀποθανοῦσα: aor. part., "upon dying"

7 (11) Notus and Zephyrus

The South and West winds discuss the transformation of Io into a heifer and her arrival in Egypt. The story of Io is told in Aeschylus' Prometheus Bound and in his Suppliants. Usually she is turned into a cow by Zeus to hide his affair, but here it is a punishment by Hera. Either way Io becomes associated with the Egyptian goddess Isis, who takes the form of a cow, as Hermes was associated with the jackal-headed Anubis.

ΝΟΤΟΣ: Ταύτην, ὦ Ζέφυρε, τὴν δάμαλιν, ἣν διὰ τοῦ πελάγους ἐς Αἴγυπτον ὁ Ἑρμῆς ἄγει, ὁ Ζεὺς διεκόρευσεν ἁλοὺς ἔρωτι;

ΖΕΦΥΡΟΣ: Ναί, ὦ Νότε· οὐ δάμαλις δὲ τότε, ἀλλὰ παῖς ἦν τοῦ ποταμοῦ Ἰνάχου· νῦν δὲ ἡ Ἥρα τοιαύτην ἐποίησεν αὐτὴν ζηλοτυπήσασα, ὅτι καὶ πάνυ ἑώρα ἐρῶντα τὸν Δία.

ΝΟΤΟΣ: Νῦν οὖν ἔτι ἐρᾷ τῆς βοός;

ἄγω: to lead or carry, to convey
Αἴγυπτος, ὁ: the river Nile, i.e. Egypt
ἁλίσκομαι: to be captured
βοῦς, ὁ: a cow
δάμαλις, -εως, ὁ: a heifer
διακορέω: to deflower
ἐράω: to love, be in love
Ἑρμῆς, -οῦ, ὁ: Hermes
ἔρως, -ωτος, ὁ: love

Ζεύς, ὁ: Zeus
Ζέφυρος, ὁ: Zephyrus, the west wind
ζηλοτυπέω: to be jealous
Ἥρα, ἡ: Hera
Ἴναχος, ὁ: Inachus, a river in Argos
παῖς, παιδός, ὁ: a child
πέλαγος, -ους, τό: the sea
ποιέω: to make
ποταμός, ὁ: a river, stream

τὴν δάμαλιν: acc. pred., "is this *the heifer*?" i.e. Io, the daughter of Inachus
διεκόρευσεν: aor., "did Zeus *deflower* her?"
ἁλοὺς: aor. part. of ἁλίσκομαι, "having been captured"
τότε: "then" i.e. when Zeus fell in love
τοῦ ποταμοῦ Ἰνάχου: gen. of source, "she was *of the river Inachus*"
τοιαύτην: acc. pred., "Hera made her *such*"
ζηλοτυπήσασα: aor. part. causal, "because she was jealous"
ἐρῶντα: pr. part. in ind. st. after ἑώρα, "she saw *that Zeus was in love*"
τῆς βοός: gen. after ἐρᾷ, "loves (her being) *a cow*"

ΖΕΦΥΡΟΣ: Καὶ μάλα, καὶ διὰ τοῦτο ἐς Αἴγυπτον αὐτὴν ἔπεμψεν καὶ ἡμῖν προσέταξε μὴ κυμαίνειν τὴν θάλατταν ἔστ' ἂν διανήξηται, ὡς ἀποτεκοῦσα ἐκεῖ — κυεῖ δὲ ἤδη — θεὸς γένοιτο καὶ αὐτὴ καὶ τὸ τεχθέν.

ΝΟΤΟΣ: Ἡ δάμαλις θεός;

ΖΕΦΥΡΟΣ: Καὶ μάλα, ὦ Νότε· ἄρξει τε, ὡς ὁ Ἑρμῆς ἔφη, τῶν πλεόντων καὶ ἡμῶν ἔσται δέσποινα, ὅντινα ἂν ἡμῶν ἐθέλῃ ἐκπέμψαι ἢ κωλῦσαι ἐπιπνεῖν.

ΝΟΤΟΣ: Θεραπευτέα τοιγαροῦν, ὦ Ζέφυρε, ἤδη δέσποινά γε οὖσα. εὐνουστέρα γὰρ ἂν οὕτως γένοιτο.

ἀποτίκτω: to bring into the world
ἄρχω: to be first, to preside over (+ gen.)
δάμαλις, -εως, ὁ: a heifer
δέσποινα, ἡ: a mistress, lady of the house
διανήχομαι: to swim across
ἐθέλω: to will, wish, purpose
ἐκεῖ: there, in that place
ἐκπέμπω: to send out or forth from
ἐπιπνέω: to breathe upon, to blow freshly upon
ἔστε: up to the time that, until
εὔνους, -ουν: well-disposed

θάλαττα, ἡ: the sea
θεός, ὁ: God
θεραπεύω: to do service to
κυέω: to be pregnant with, bear in the womb
κυμαίνω: to rise in waves or billows, to swell
κωλύω: to let, hinder, check, prevent
μάλα: very
πέμπω: to send
πλέω: to sail, go by sea
προστάττω: to order (+ inf.)
τίκτω: to give birth
τοιγαροῦν: so then, wherefore, therefore,

μὴ κυμαίνειν: pr. inf. in ind. com. after προσέταξε, "he ordered us *not to swell* the sea"

ἔστε ἂν διανήξηται: aor. subj. in gen. temp. cl., "until she swims across" (whenever that is)

ἀποτεκοῦσα: aor. part., "once she has given birth"

ὡς ... γένοιτο: aor. opt. in purpose cl., "in order that she become a god"

τὸ τεχθέν: aor. part. pass. also the subj. of γένοιτο, "both she and *the one having been born*" i.e. the child

τῶν πλεόντων: pr. part. gen. after ἄρξει, "she will rule *those sailing*"

ὅντινα ἂν ... ἐθέλῃ: pr. subj. in gen. relative cl., "*whomever* of us *she wishes to*" + inf.

ἐκπέμψαι ἢ κωλῦσαι: aor. inf. complementing ἐθέλῃ, "to send forth or to hinder"

ἐπιπνεῖν: pr. inf. after κωλῦσαι, "to hinder *from blowing*"

θεραπευτέα (sc. ἐστι): verbal adj. nom. s. f. in periphrastic, "she ought to be served"

ἂν οὕτως γένοιτο: pot. aor. opt., "*she would thus be* more well-disposed."

ΖΕΦΥΡΟΣ: Ἀλλ' ἤδη γὰρ διεπέρασε καὶ ἐξένευσεν ἐς τὴν γῆν. ὁρᾷς ὅπως οὐκέτι μὲν τετραποδητὶ βαδίζει, ἀνορθώσας δὲ αὐτὴν ὁ Ἑρμῆς γυναῖκα παγκάλην αὖθις ἐποίησε;

ΝΟΤΟΣ: Παράδοξα γοῦν ταῦτα, ὦ Ζέφυρε· οὐκέτι τὰ κέρατα οὐδὲ οὐρὰ καὶ δίχηλα τὰ σκέλη, ἀλλ' ἐπέραστος κόρη. ὁ μέντοι Ἑρμῆς τί παθὼν μεταβέβληκεν ἑαυτὸν καὶ ἀντὶ νεανίου κυνοπρόσωπος γεγένηται;

ΖΕΦΥΡΟΣ: Μὴ πολυπραγμονῶμεν, ὅτι ἄμεινον ἐκεῖνος οἶδε τὰ πρακτέα.

ἀμείνων, -ον: better, abler, stronger, braver
ἀνορθόω: to stand straight up
ἀντὶ: in place of (+ *gen*.)
βαδίζω: to go slowly, to walk
γῆ, ἡ: earth, shore
διαπεράω: to go over or across
δίχηλος, -ον: cloven-hoofed
ἐκνέω: to swim out, swim to land, escape by swimming
ἐπέραστος, -ον: lovely, amiable
κέρας, -ατος, τό: a horn
κόρη, ἡ: a maiden
κυνοπρόσωπος, -ον: dog-faced

μεταβάλλω: to change, alter
νεανίας, -ου, ὁ: a youth
οἶδα: to know
οὐρά, ἡ: a tail
πάγκαλος, -η, -ον: all beautiful, good or noble
παράδοξος, -ον: paradoxical
πάσχω: to suffer
πολυπραγμονέω: to be inquisitive or meddlesome
πράττω: to do
σκέλος, -εος, τό: a leg
τετραποδητί: on all fours

ἐξένευσεν: aor., "*she swam out* onto the shore"
ὅπως ... βαδίζει: ind. quest. after ὁρᾷς, "see *how she no longer walks*"
ἀνορθώσας: aor. part., "Hermes, *having straightened her up*"
γυναῖκα: acc. pred. after ἐποίησεν, "he made her *a woman*"
τί παθὼν: aor. part. causal, "suffering what?" i.e. what caused him? why?
μεταβέβληκεν: perf. of μετα-βάλλω, "why *has he changed* himself?"
γεγένηται: perf., "he has become"
κυνοπρόσωπος: "dog-faced" as Io was associated with the Egyptian Isis, Hermes was associated with the jackal-headed Anubis.
μὴ πολυπραγμονῶμεν: pr. subj. jussive, "let us not be inquisitive"
τὰ πρακτέα: verbal adj. of πράττω, "the things which must be done"

8 (5) Poseidon and the Dolphins

The story of Arion, the Methymnean poet who is saved by dolphins from greedy pirates, is told in Herodotus 1, 23-4. It is retold here from the standpoint of the dolphins themselves, whose care for mankind is accounted for by the fact that they themselves were once men, who were changed to dolphins by Dionysus. That story is told in the Homeric Hymn to Dionysus. Brief reference is made to the earlier help the dolphins provided to Melicertes, the son of Ino, when he leapt into the sea.

ΠΟΣΕΙΔΩΝ: Εὖ γε, ὦ Δελφῖνες, ὅτι ἀεὶ φιλάνθρωποί ἐστε, καὶ πάλαι μὲν τὸ τῆς Ἰνοῦς παιδίον ἐπὶ τὸν Ἰσθμὸν ἐκομίσατε ὑποδεξάμενοι ἀπὸ τῶν Σκειρωνίδων μετὰ τῆς μητρὸς ἐμπεσόν, καὶ νῦν σὺ τὸν κιθαρῳδὸν τουτονὶ τὸν ἐκ Μηθύμνης ἀναλαβὼν ἐξενήξω ἐς Ταίναρον

ἀναλαμβάνω: to take up, take into one's hands
δελφίς, -ῖνος, ὁ: a dolphin
ἐκνήχομαι: to swim out or away
ἐμπίπτω: to fall upon
Ἰνώ, -οῦς, ἡ: Ino, a daughter of Cadmus
Ἰσθμός, ὁ: Isthmus of Corinth
κιθαρῳδός, ὁ: a cithara player, harper
κομίζω: to take care of, to convey to
Μηθύμνη, ἡ: Methymna, a city on Lesbos

μήτηρ, μητρός, ἡ: a mother
παιδίον, τό: a child
πάλαι: long ago
Σκειρωνίδες (sc. πέτραι): the Scironian rocks near the Isthmus of Corinth
Ταίναρος, ἡ: Taenarus, on the southern tip of the Peloponnese
ὑποδέχομαι: to receive beneath
φιλάνθρωπος, -ον: loving mankind, humane, benevolent

τῆς Ἰνοῦς παιδίον: Ino, one of the daughters of Cadmus, pursued by her crazed husband, leapt into the sea with her son Melicertes. Both were deified. Ino became Leucothea, who figures in the fifth book of the *Odyssey*; Melicertes the sea-god Palaemon, mentioned first in Euripides' *Iphigeneia in Tauris*.

ὑποδεξάμενοι: aor. part., "having received"

τῶν Σκειρωνίδων (sc. πετρῶν): "from the Scironian (cliffs)"

ἐμπεσόν: aor. part. n. agreeing with παιδίον, "having fallen"

τὸν κιθαρῳδόν: the musician is Arion

ἀναλαβών: aor. part., "having taken up"

ἐξενήξω: aor. 2 s. of ἐκ-νήχομαι, "you swam away"

Lucian

αὐτῇ σκευῇ καὶ κιθάρᾳ, οὐδὲ περιεῖδες κακῶς ὑπὸ τῶν ναυτῶν ἀπολλύμενον.

ἀπόλλυμι: to destroy utterly, kill, slay
κακός, -ή, -όν: bad
κιθάρα, ἡ: a cithara, a stringed instrument

ναύτης, -ου, ὁ: a sailor
σκευή, ἡ: equipment

αὐτῇ σκευῇ καὶ κιθάρᾳ: dat., "even with his gear and cithara," i.e. with gear and all
περιεῖδες: aor. of περι-οράω, "you did not overlook" i.e. allow
ἀπολλύμενον: pr. part. in ind. st. after περιεῖδες, "you did not allow him *to be destroyed*"
ὑπὸ τῶν ναυτῶν: "at the hands of the sailors"

αὐτός again

1. Besides the uses of **αὐτός** indicated above (p. 25), this word also combines with pronouns to form reflexive pronouns:

    ἐμ- αυτόν, ἐμ- αυτήν: myself

    σε- αυτόν, σε- αυτήν: yourself; also Ἰνὼ πείσεταιόν, σαυτήν

    ἑ- αυτόν, ἑ- αυτήν: himself, herself

    Similarly in the plural:

    ἡμάς αὐτούς; ὑμάς αὐτούς; ἑ- αὐτούς

    The only difficulty is that the third person forms based on the pronoun ἑ- often coalesce with the first syllable of **αὐτόν**, producing a crasis that looks like the simple form of **αὐτόν**, except for the breathing mark:

    ἑ- αυτόν — αὑτόν

    ἑ- αυτήν — αὑτήν

    ἑ- αὐτούς — αὑτούς

2. The definite article can also contract with **αὐτός**:

    ὁ αὐτός — αὑτός

    ἡ αὐτή — αὑτή:

    τὸ αὐτό — ταὐτό

    These all mean "the same." Distinguish from **τοῦτο** "this one" and **ταῦτα** "these ones"

3. Note also the idiomatic use of the dative case when used with a noun:

    τουτονὶ τὸν ἐκ Μηθύμνης ἀναλαβὼν ἐξενήξω ἐς Ταίναρον αὐτῇ σκευῇ: "Having taken up this man, the one from Methymna, you swam him to Taenarum, *equipment and all*."

ΔΕΛΦΙΝΕΣ: Μὴ θαυμάσῃς, ὦ Πόσειδον, εἰ τοὺς ἀνθρώπους εὖ ποιοῦμεν, ἐξ ἀνθρώπων γε καὶ αὐτοὶ ἰχθύες γενόμενοι.

ΠΟΣΕΙΔΩΝ: Καὶ μέμφομαί γε τῷ Διονύσῳ, ὅτι ὑμᾶς καταναυμαχήσας μετέβαλε, δέον χειρώσασθαι μόνον, ὥσπερ τοὺς ἄλλους ὑπηγάγετο. πῶς δ' οὖν τὰ κατὰ τὸν Ἀρίονα τοῦτον ἐγένετο, ὦ Δελφίν;

ΔΕΛΦΙΝΕΣ: Ὁ Περίανδρος, οἶμαι, ἔχαιρεν αὐτῷ καὶ πολλάκις μετεπέμπετο αὐτὸν ἐπὶ τῇ τέχνῃ, ὁ δὲ πλουτήσας παρὰ τοῦ τυράννου ἐπεθύμησε πλεύσας οἴκαδε ἐς τὴν

ἄνθρωπος, ὁ: a man
Ἀρίων, -ονος, ὁ: Arion the poet
Διόνυσος, ὁ: Dionysus
ἐπιθυμέω: to desire
θαυμάζω: to wonder, marvel, be astonished
ἰχθύς, ὁ: a fish
καταναυμαχέω: to conquer in a sea-fight
μέμφομαι: to blame (+ dat.)
μεταβάλλω: to turn quickly, to change
μεταπέμπω: to send after
μόνον: only

οἴκαδε: homewards
οἶμαι: to suppose, think
Περίανδρος, ὁ: Periander, tyrant of Corinth
πλέω: to sail, go by sea
πλουτέω: to be rich, wealthy
Ποσειδῶν, -ῶνος, ὁ: Poseidon
τέχνη, ἡ: art, skill
τύραννος, ὁ: an absolute sovereign
ὑπάγω: to lead or bring under
χαίρω: to rejoice, to be delighted in (+ dat.)
χειρόω: to subdue

μὴ θαυμάσῃς: aor. subj. in prohibition, "don't wonder!"
γενόμενοι: aor. part. causal, "since we ourselves became"
ὅτι ... μετέβαλε: aor. of μετα-βάλλω, "because he changed you"
καταναυμαχήσας: aor. part., "having conquered you in a sea-battle"
δέον: pr. part. of δεῖ used absolutely, "it being necessary" + inf.
χειρώσασθαι: aor. inf. mid. after δέον, "necessary only *to subdue*"
ὑπηγάγετο: aor. of ὑπο-ἄγω, "just as *he subjected* others"
τὰ κατὰ τὸν: "*the things about* Arion"
πῶς ... ἐγένετο: aor., "how did they happen?"
ἔχαιρεν: impf. 3s. of χαίρω, "he rejoiced"
ἐπὶ τῇ τέχνῃ: "on account of his skill"
ὁ δὲ: "but he" i.e. Arion
πλουτήσας: aor. part., "having become rich"
πλεύσας: aor. part. of πλέω, instr., "he wished *by sailing*"

Μήθυμναν ἐπιδείξασθαι τὸν πλοῦτον, καὶ ἐπιβὰς πορ-
θμείου τινὸς κακούργων ἀνδρῶν ὡς ἔδειξε πολὺν ἄγων
χρυσόν τε καὶ ἄργυρον, ἐπεὶ κατὰ μέσον τὸ Αἰγαῖον ἐγένετο, ἐπιβουλεύουσιν αὐτῷ οἱ ναῦται· ὁ δὲ — ἠκροώμην
γὰρ ἅπαντα παρανέων τῷ σκάφει — «Ἐπεὶ ταῦτα ὑμῖν
δέδοκται,» ἔφη, «ἀλλὰ τὴν σκευὴν ἀναλαβόντα με καὶ
ᾄσαντα θρῆνόν τινα ἐπ' ἐμαυτῷ ἑκόντα ἐάσατε ῥῖψαι
ἐμαυτόν.» ἐπέτρεψαν οἱ ναῦται καὶ ἀνέλαβε τὴν σκευὴν

ἄγω: to lead or carry, to convey, bring
ᾄδω: to sing
Αἰγαῖος, -α, -ον: Aegean
ἀκροάομαι: to listen to
ἀναλαμβάνω: to take up, take into one's hands
ἀνήρ, ἀνδρός ὁ: a man
ἅπας, ἅπασα, ἅπαν: all, every, whole
ἄργυρος, ὁ: silver
δείκνυμι: to bring to light, display, exhibit
δοκέω: to seem (good)
ἑκών: willing, of free will, readily
ἐπιβαίνω: to go upon
ἐπιβουλεύω: to plan or contrive against
ἐπιδείκνυμι: to display

ἐπιτρέπω: to turn towards, to agree to
θρῆνος, ὁ: a funeral-song, dirge, lament
κακοῦργος, -ον: mischievous, knavish
μέσος, -η, -ον: middle, in the middle
Μήθυμνα, ἡ: Methymna, a city on the island of Lesbos.
ναύτης, -ου, ὁ: a sailor
παρανέω: to swim beside (+ dat.)
πλοῦτος, ὁ: wealth
πορθμεῖον, τό: a ferry boat
ῥίπτω: to throw, cast, hurl
σκάφος, -εος, τό: ship, boat
σκευῆ, ἡ: equipment
χρυσός, ὁ: gold

ἐπιδείξασθαι: aor. inf. compl. ἐπεθύμησεν, "wished *to show*"
ἐπιβάς: aor. part., "having got on board" + gen.
ἄγων: pr. part. in ind. st. after ἔδειξε, "because he revealed *that he was leading*"
ἐπιβουλεύουσιν: note the sudden change in tense and subject, "the sailors begin plotting against him"
ὁ δὲ: "but he" i.e. Arion
ἠκροώμην: impf. of ἀκροάομαι, in a parenthetical statement, "for I was listening"
παρανέων: pr. part., "swimming beside"
ἐπεὶ ... δέδοκται: perf., "since these things have seemed good" i.e. since it has been decided
ἀναλαβόντα με καὶ ᾄσαντα: aor. part. acc. s., "me, having taken up and having sung"
ἑκόντα: pr. part. also agreeing with με, "willingly"
ῥῖψαι: aor. inf. of ῥίπτω after ἐάσατε, "allow me *to throw* myself"
ἐπέτρεψαν οἱ ναῦται καὶ ἀνέλαβε: note again the sharp change of subject, "the sailors agreed and he took up"

καὶ ᾖσε πάνυ λιγυρόν, καὶ ἔπεσεν ἐς τὴν θάλατταν ὡς αὐτίκα πάντως ἀποθανούμενος· ἐγὼ δὲ ὑπολαβὼν καὶ ἀναθέμενος αὐτὸν ἐξενηξάμην ἔχων εἰς Ταίναρον.

ΠΟΣΕΙΔΩΝ: Ἐπαινῶ σε τῆς φιλομουσίας· ἄξιον γὰρ τὸν μισθὸν ἀποδέδωκας αὐτῷ τῆς ἀκροάσεως.

Dionysus and the Dolphins,
black figure kylix *by Exekias (c. 540 BCE)*

ᾄδω: to sing
ἀκρόασις, -εως, ἡ: a hearing or listening
ἀνατίθημι: to lay upon
ἄξιος, -ία, -ον: worthy
ἀποδίδωμι: to give back to X (*dat.*) in exchange for Y (*gen.*)
ἀποθνῄσκω: to die
αὐτίκα: at once
ἐκνήχομαι: to swim out or away

ἐπαινέω: to approve, applaud, commend
θάλαττα, ἡ: the sea
λιγυρός, -ά, -όν: clear
μισθός, ὁ: wages, award
πάντως: altogether;
πίπτω: to fall, fall down
ὑπολαμβάνω: to take up by getting under
φιλομουσία, ἡ: a love of music

ᾖσε: aor. of ᾄδω, "he sang"
πάνυ λιγυρόν: adverbial acc., "very clearly"
ἔπεσεν: aor. of πίπτω, "he fell"
ὡς ... ἀποθανούμενος: fut. part. indicating alleged purpose, "in order to die"
ὑπολαβών: aor. part., "having taken up"
ἀναθέμενος: aor. part., "having laid him (upon me)"
ἐξενηξάμην: aor. of ἐκ-νήχομαι, "I swam out"
ἔχων: pr. part., "carrying him"
ἄξιον: acc. pred., "a pay *that is worthy*"
ἀποδέδωκας: perf. of ἀποδίδωμι, "you have given back"

9 (6) Poseidon and the Nereids

Poseidon and Amphitrite discuss the recent death of Helle, who drowned in the sea subsequently named for her, the Hellespont. She and her brother Phrixus were attacked by their stepmother, Ino, but were saved by their own mother, Nephele. Nephele sent them to Colchis on the back of a golden ram, a gift from Hermes. Poseidon also alludes to the fate of Ino at the end, linking this dialogue to 7 above. Amphitrite wonders out loud why Helle must die and why the wicked Ino should be saved later, questions that Poseidon tactfully answers.

ΠΟΣΕΙΔΩΝ: Τὸ μὲν στενὸν τοῦτο, ἔνθα ἡ παῖς κατηνέχθη, Ἑλλήσποντος ἀπ' αὐτῆς καλείσθω· τὸν δὲ νεκρὸν ὑμεῖς, ὦ Νηρεΐδες, παραλαβοῦσαι τῇ Τρῳάδι προσενέγκατε, ὡς ταφείη ὑπὸ τῶν ἐπιχωρίων.

ΑΜΦΙΤΡΙΤΗ: Μηδαμῶς, ὦ Πόσειδον, ἀλλ' ἐνταῦθα ἐν τῷ ἐπωνύμῳ πελάγει τεθάφθω· ἐλεοῦμεν γὰρ αὐτὴν οἴκτιστα ὑπὸ τῆς μητρυιᾶς πεπονθυῖαν.

ἐλεέω: to have pity on
Ἑλλήσποντος, ὁ: the Hellespont, sea of Helle
ἐπιχώριος, ὁ: a native
ἐπώνυμος, -ον: given as a name, eponymous
θάπτω: to bury
καλέω: to call
καταφέρω: to bring down
μηδαμῶς: in no way, not at all
μητρυιά, -ᾶς, ἡ: a step-mother
νεκρός, ὁ: a dead body, corpse

οἴκτιστος, -η, -ον: most pitiable, lamentable
παῖς, παιδός, ἡ: a child
παραλαμβάνω: to receive from
πάσχω: to suffer
πέλαγος, -ους, τό: the sea
Ποσειδῶν, -ῶνος, ὁ: Poseidon
προσφέρω: to bring to or upon, to convey
στενόν, τό: a narrow place, a strait
Τρῳάς, -άδος, ἡ: the Troad

κατηνέχθη: aor. pass. of κατα-φέρω, "was brought down"
Ἑλλήσποντος: Helles, daughter of Athamas and Nephele, was drowned in the Hellespont.
ἀπ' αὐτῆς: "after her"
καλείσθω: pr. imper. 3 s., "let it be called"
παραλαβοῦσαι: aor. part., "you, having taken up"
προσενέγκατε: aor. imper. of προσφέρω, "convey it!"
ὡς ταφείη: aor. opt. pass. of θάπτω in purp. cl., "so that it may be buried."
τεθάφθω: perf. imper. of θάπτω, "let her be buried"
πεπονθυῖαν: perf. part. of πάσχω, "her *having suffered*"

ΠΟΣΕΙΔΩΝ: Τοῦτο μέν, ὦ Ἀμφιτρίτη, οὐ θέμις: οὐδὲ ἄλλως καλὸν ἐνταῦθά που κεῖσθαι ὑπὸ τῇ ψάμμῳ αὐτήν, ἀλλ᾽ ὅπερ ἔφην ἐν τῇ Τρῳάδι ἢ ἐν Χερρονήσῳ τεθάψεται. ἐκεῖνο δὲ παραμύθιον οὐ μικρὸν ἔσται αὐτῇ, ὅτι μετ᾽ ὀλίγον τὰ αὐτὰ καὶ ἡ Ἰνὼ πείσεται, καὶ ἐμπεσεῖται ὑπὸ τοῦ Ἀθάμαντος διωκομένη ἐς τὸ πέλαγος ἀπ᾽ ἄκρου τοῦ Κιθαιρῶνος, καθ᾽ ὅπερ καθήκει ἐς τὴν θάλατταν, ἔχουσα καὶ τὸν υἱὸν ἐπὶ τῆς ἀγκάλης. ἀλλὰ κἀκείνην σῶσαι δεήσει χαρισαμένους τῷ Διονύσῳ: τροφὸς γὰρ αὐτοῦ καὶ τίτθη ἡ Ἰνώ.

ἀγκάλη, ἡ: an arm
Ἀθάμας, -αντος, ὁ: Athamas, husband of Ino
ἄκρον, -ον, τό: the highest or furthest point
ἄλλως: in another way or manner
Ἀμφιτρίτη, ἡ: Amphitrite
Διόνυσος, ὁ: Dionysus
διώκω: to pursue
ἐμπίπτω: to fall upon
θάλαττα, ἡ: the sea
θάπτω: to bury
θέμις, ἡ: a law, custom
Ἰνώ, -οῦς, ἡ: Ino
καθήκω: to go down
καλός, -η, -ον: beautiful
κεῖμαι: to be laid
Κιθαιρών, -ῶνος, ὁ: Mt. Cithaeon

μικρός, -ά, -όν: small, little
ὀλίγος, -η, -ον: few, little, scanty, small
παραμύθιον, τό: a comfort
πάσχω: to suffer
πέλαγος, -ους, τό: the sea
σῴζω: to save
τίτθη, ἡ: a nurse
τροφός, ὁ: a feeder, rearer, nurse
Τρῳάς, -άδος, ἡ: the Troad, the Asian side of the opening to the Black Sea
υἱός, ὁ: a son
χαρίζομαι: to please
Χερρόνησος, ἡ: the Chersonese, i.e. the Thracian Chersonese or peninsula opposite the Troad on the European side of the opening to the Black Sea
ψάμμος, ἡ: sand

κεῖσθαι: pr. inf. epex. after **καλὸν**, "a good thing for her *to be laid*"
ὅπερ ἔφην: parenthetical, "as I said"
τεθάψεται: fut. perf., "she will be buried"
μετ᾽ ὀλίγον (sc. **χρόνον**): "after a little while"
ὅτι … πείσεται: fut. of **πάσχω** in noun cl. in app. to **ἐκεῖνο**, "that, namely *that Ino will suffer*"
ἐμπεσεῖται: fut. of **ἐμπίπτω**, "and she will fall into"
καθ᾽ ὅπερ (=κατὰ ὅπερ): "in the very spot which"
ἔχουσα: pr. part., "she *holding*"
κἀκείνην (= καί ἐκείνην): "to save *that one too*"
σῶσαι: aor. inf. complementing **δεήσει**, "it will be necessary for us *to save*"
χαρισαμένους: aor. part. acc. agreeing with the subj. of **σῶσαι** expressing purpose, "in order to please" + dat.

ΑΜΦΙΤΡΙΤΗ: Οὐκ ἐχρῆν οὕτω πονηρὰν οὖσαν.

ΠΟΣΕΙΔΩΝ: Ἀλλὰ τῷ Διονύσῳ ἀχαριστεῖν, ὦ Ἀμφιτρίτη, οὐκ ἄξιον.

ΝΗΡΕΙΔΕΣ: Αὕτη δὲ ἄρα τί παθοῦσα κατέπεσεν ἀπὸ τοῦ κριοῦ, ὁ ἀδελφὸς δὲ ὁ Φρίξος ἀσφαλῶς ὀχεῖται;

ΠΟΣΕΙΔΩΝ: Εἰκότως: νεανίας γὰρ καὶ δύνατος ἀντέχειν πρὸς τὴν φοράν, ἡ δὲ ὑπ᾽ ἀηθείας ἐπιβᾶσα ὀχήματος παραδόξου καὶ ἀπιδοῦσα ἐς βάθος ἀχανές, ἐκπλαγεῖσα

ἀδελφός, ὁ: a brother
ἀήθεια, ἡ: unaccustomedness
Ἀμφιτρίτη, ἡ: Amphitrite
ἀντέχω: to hold against
ἄξιος, -ία, -ον: worthy
ἄρα: then and there
ἀσφαλῶς: safely
ἀχανής, -ές: gaping
ἀχαριστέω: to be thankless, show ingratitude
βάθος, τό: a depth, height
δύνατος, -η, -ον: able to (+ *inf.*)
εἰκότως: naturally
ἐκπλήττω: to drive out of one's sense, to be astounded

ἐπιβαίνω: to go upon
καταπίπτω: to fall or drop down
κριός, ὁ: a ram
νεανίας, -ου, ὁ: a young man, a youth
ὀχέω: to uphold, sustain, endure
ὄχημα, -ατος, τό: a means of conveyance, vehicle
παράδοξος, -ον: paradoxical
πονηρός, -ά, -όν: toilsome, painful
φορά, ἡ: a carrying, the journey
Φρίξος, ὁ: Phrixus
χρή: it is necessary

ἐχρῆν: impf. of χρή, "it was not necessary (to save)"
οὖσαν: pr. part. circumstantial, "(a woman) *who was so bad*"
ἀχαριστεῖν: pr. inf. epex. after ἄξιον, "not worthy *to show ingratitude*"
τί παθοῦσα: aor. part. instrumental, "by suffering what?"
κατέπεσεν: aor. of κατα-πίπτω, "did she (i.e. Helle) fall?"
Φρίξος: Phrixus was the son of Athamas and the twin brother of Helle.
ἀντέχειν: pr. inf. after δύνατος, "able *to hold against*"
ἡ δέ: "but she" i.e. Helle
ἐπιβᾶσα: aor. part., "having stepped upon" + gen.
ἀπιδοῦσα: aor. part. of ἀπο-ὁράω, "having looked down"
ἐκπλαγεῖσα: aor. pass. part. of ἐκπλήσσω, "having been astounded"

καὶ τῷ θάλπει ἅμα συσχεθεῖσα καὶ ἰλιγγιάσασα πρὸς τὸ σφοδρὸν τῆς πτήσεως ἀκρατὴς ἐγένετο τῶν κεράτων τοῦ κριοῦ, ὧν τέως ἐπείληπτο, καὶ κατέπεσεν ἐς τὸ πέλαγος.

ΝΗΡΕΙΔΕΣ: Οὔκουν ἐχρῆν τὴν μητέρα τὴν Νεφέλην βοηθῆσαι πιπτούσῃ;

ΠΟΣΕΙΔΩΝ: Ἐχρῆν· ἀλλ' ἡ Μοῖρα τῆς Νεφέλης πολλῷ δυνατωτέρα.

ἀκρατής, -ές: powerless, impotent
ἅμα: at the same time
βοηθέω: to help (+ dat.)
δυνατός, -ή, -όν: able, strong
ἐπιλαμβάνω: to lay hold of, seize, attack
θάλπος, -εος, τό: warmth, heat
ἰλιγγιάω: to become dizzy
καταπίπτω: to fall or drop down
κέρας, -ατος, τό: a horn
κριός, ὁ: a ram

μήτηρ, μητρός, ἡ: a mother
Μοῖρα, ἡ: Fate
Νεφέλη, ἡ: Nephele
πέλαγος, -ους, τό: the sea
πίπτω: to fall, fall down
πτῆσις, -εως, ἡ: a flying, flight
συνέχομαι: to be afflicted
σφοδρός, τό: violence
τέως: so long, up to that time
χρή: it is necessary

τῷ θάλπει: dat. means, "afflicted *by the heat*"
συσχεθεῖσα: aor. part pass. of συν-έχομαι, "she *having been afflicted*"
ἰλιγγιάσασα: aor. part., "having grown dizzy"
πτήσεως: gen. after σφοδρὸν, "from the violence *of the flight*"
ἀκρατὴς: nom. pred., "she became powerless" + gen., i.e. she lost hold of the horns
ἐπείληπτο: plupf. of ἐπι-λαμβάνω, "which *she had seized*"
κατέπεσεν: aor. from κατα-πίπτω, "she fell"
βοηθῆσαι: aor. inf. after ἐχρῆν, "necessary for her mother *to help*"
πιπτούσῃ: pr. part. dat., "help her *falling*"
πολλῷ: dat. of degree of difference, "stronger *by much*"

10 (9) Iris and Poseidon

The subject of this dialogue is the establishment of the wandering island of Delos in its permanent location so that Leto can deliver her famous twin deities. The episode is told in the Homeric Hymn to Apollo and in Callimachus' Hymn to Delos. Poseidon is represented executing the will of his brother Zeus.

ΙΡΙΣ: Τὴν νῆσον τὴν πλανωμένην, ὦ Πόσειδον, ἣν ἀποσπασθεῖσαν τῆς Σικελίας ὕφαλον ἔτι νήχεσθαι συμβέβηκε, ταύτην, φησὶν ὁ Ζεύς, στῆσον ἤδη καὶ ἀνάφηνον καὶ ποίησον ἤδη δῆλον ἐν τῷ Αἰγαίῳ μέσῳ βεβαίως μένειν στηρίξας πάνυ ἀσφαλῶς· δεῖται γάρ τι αὐτῆς.

Αἰγαῖος, -α, -ον: Aegean
ἀναφαίνω: to make visible
ἀποσπάω: to tear or drag away from (+ gen.)
ἀσφαλής, -ές: not liable to fall, immoveable
βέβαιος, -ον: firm, steady, steadfast, sure, certain
δέομαι: to have a need for (+ gen.)
δῆλος, -ον: visible, conspicuous
Ζεύς, ὁ: Zeus
ἵστημι: to make to stand
μένω: to stay, remain

μέσος, -η, -ον: middle, in the middle
νῆσος, ἡ: an island
νήχομαι: to swim
πλανάομαι: to wander
ποιέω: to make
Ποσειδῶν, -ῶνος, ὁ: Poseidon
Σικελία, -ου, ἡ: Sicily
στηρίζω: to make fast, prop, fix, set
συμβαίνω: to come to pass
ὕφαλος, -ον: under the sea

τὴν νῆσον: acc. obj. of στῆσον below, "fix in place *the wandering island*."
ἀποσπασθεῖσαν: aor. part. pass., "having been dragged away from"
νήχεσθαι: pr. inf. after συμβέβηκεν, "it has come to pass that the island *is swimming*"
συμβέβηκεν: perf. impers., "it has come to pass that" + acc. + inf.
στῆσον: aor. imper. of ἵστημι, "make it stand!"
ἀνάφηνον: aor. imper., "make it visible!"
δῆλον: acc. pred. after ποίησον, "make it *visible*," punning on the name Δῆλος
μένειν: pr. inf. after στηρίξας, "having fixed it *to remain*"
στηρίξας: aor. part., "having fixed it."
δεῖται: pr., "something is needed" + gen.

50

ΠΟΣΕΙΔΩΝ: Πεπράξεται ταῦτα, ὦ Ἶρι. τίνα δ' ὅμως παρέξει αὐτῷ τὴν χρείαν ἀναφανεῖσα καὶ μηκέτι πλέουσα;

ΙΡΙΣ: Τὴν Λητὼ ἐπ' αὐτῆς δεῖ ἀποκυῆσαι· ἤδη δὲ πονήρως ὑπὸ τῶν ὠδίνων ἔχει.

ΠΟΣΕΙΔΩΝ: Τί οὖν; οὐχ ἱκανὸς ὁ οὐρανὸς ἐντεκεῖν; εἰ δὲ μὴ οὗτος, ἀλλ' ἥ γε γῆ πᾶσα οὐκ ἂν δύναιτο ὑποδέξασθαι τὰς γονὰς αὐτῆς;

ΙΡΙΣ: Οὔκ, ὦ Πόσειδον· ἡ Ἥρα γὰρ ὅρκῳ μεγάλῳ κατέλαβε τὴν γῆν, μὴ παρασχεῖν τῇ Λητοῖ τῶν ὠδίνων ὑποδοχήν. ἡ τοίνυν νῆσος αὕτη ἀνώμοτός ἐστιν· ἀφανὴς γὰρ ἦν.

ἀναφαίνω: to make visible
ἀνώμοτος, -ον: unsworn, not bound by oath
ἀποκυέω: to bear young, bring forth
ἀφανής, -ές: unseen, invisible
γῆ, ἡ: earth
γονή, ἡ: produce, offspring
δύναμαι: to be able, capable (+ inf.)
ἐντίκτω: to bear or produce in
Ἥρα, ἡ: Hera
ἱκανός, -η, -ον: becoming, befitting, sufficing
Ἶρις, -ιδος, ἡ: Iris
καταλαμβάνω: to lay hold of, bind
Λητώ, -οῦς, ἡ: Leto, mother of Apollo and Artemis
νῆσος, ἡ: an island
ὅρκος, ὁ: an oath
οὐρανός, ὁ: heaven
παρέχω: to furnish, provide X (acc.) for Y (dat.)
πλέω: to sail, go by sea
πονηρός, -ά, -όν: toilsome, painful, grievous
πράττω: to do
τοίνυν: therefore, accordingly
ὑποδέχομαι: to receive
ὑποδοχή, ἡ: a reception for (+ gen.)
χρεία, ἡ: a use, advantage, service
ὠδίς, -ῖνος: the pangs or throes of labour

πεπράξεται: fut. perf. of πράττω, "it will have been done"
παρέξει: fut., "what need *will it provide?*"
ἀναφανεῖσα: aor. pass., "having become visible"
ἐπ' αὐτῆς: "upon it."
ἀποκυῆσαι: aor. inf. after δεῖ, "necessary *to give birth*"
πονήρως ... ἔχει: "she is grievous"
ὑπὸ τῶν ὠδίνων: "from the pains of labor," using the agency expression
ἐντεκεῖν: aor. inf. epex. after ἱκανός, "sufficient *to bear*"
ἂν ... δύναιτο: pr. opt. pot., "would not the earth be able to?" + inf.
κατέλαβε: aor. ind. act. of καταλαμβάνω, "*she bound* the earth"
μὴ παρασχεῖν: aor. inf. in ind. com., "with an oath *not to provide*"

ΠΟΣΕΙΔΩΝ: Συνίημι. στῆθι, ὦ νῆσε, καὶ ἀνάδυθι αὖθις ἐκ τοῦ βυθοῦ καὶ μηκέτι ὑποφέρου, ἀλλὰ βεβαίως μένε καὶ ὑπόδεξαι, ὦ εὐδαιμονεστάτη, τοῦ ἀδελφοῦ τὰ τέκνα δύο, τοὺς καλλίστους τῶν θεῶν· καὶ ὑμεῖς, ὦ Τρίτωνες, διαπορθμεύσατε τὴν Λητὼ ἐς αὐτήν· καὶ γαληνὰ ἅπαντα ἔστω. τὸν δράκοντα δέ, ὃς νῦν ἐξοιστρεῖ αὐτὴν φοβῶν, τὰ νεογνὰ ἐπειδὰν τεχθῇ, αὐτίκα μέτεισι καὶ τιμωρήσει τῇ μητρί. σὺ δὲ ἀπάγγελλε τῷ Διὶ πάντα εἶναι εὐτρεπῆ· ἕστηκεν ἡ Δῆλος· ἡκέτω ἡ Λητὼ ἤδη καὶ τικτέτω.

ἀδελφός, ὁ: a brother
ἀναδύω: to come to the top of water
ἀπαγγέλλω: to bring tidings, report, announce
αὐτίκα: at once
βέβαιος, -α, -ον: firm, steady, steadfast, sure
βυθός, ὁ: a depth, height
γαληνός, -ή, -όν: calm
διαπορθμεύω: to carry over, give passage
δράκων, -οντος, ὁ: a dragon
ἐξοιστράω: to make wild, madden
ἐπειδάν: whenever (+ *subj.*)
εὐδαίμων, -ον: blessed
εὐτρεπής, -ές: readily turning, in good order

ἥκω: to have come, be present, be here
ἵστημι: to make to stand
μένω: to stay where one is, remain
μετέρχομαι: to pursue
μήτηρ, μητρός, ἡ: a mother
συνίημι: to understand
τέκνον, τό: a child
τίκτω: to bring into the world
τιμωρέω: to take vengeance, punish
Τρίτων, -ωνος, ὁ: Triton
ὑποδέχομαι: to receive beneath
ὑποφέρω: to carry away under
φοβέω: to terrify

στῆθι: aor. imper., "stay still!"
ἀνάδυθι: aor. imper., "come up!"
μηκέτι ὑποφέρου: pr. imper., "no longer drift under the surface!"
ὑπόδεξαι: aor. imper., "receive!"
τοῦ ἀδελφοῦ: gen., *my brother's* children"
διαπορθμεύσατε: aor. imper., "give passage!"
ἔστω: pr. imper., "let all be calm!"
φοβῶν: pr. part. instr., " by scaring her"
ἐπειδὰν τεχθῇ: aor. subj. pass. in gen. temp. cl., "whenever they are born"
μέτεισι καὶ τιμωρήσει: fut., "the newborns *will pursue and punish*"
τῇ μητρί: dat. of advant., "for their mother"
πάντα εἶναι: ind. st. after ἀπάγγελλε, "announce *that all things are*"
ἕστηκεν: perf. of ἵστημι, "Delos has been set up" i.e. is now standing
ἡκέτω: 3rd s. pr. imper., "let Leto come"
τικτέτω: 3rd s. pr. imper., "let her give birth"

11 (10) Xanthus and the Sea

The river Xanthus rose up against Achilles in book 21 of the Iliad, and was on the point of overwhelming him when Hephaestus rescued Achilles, scorching the river in the process. Lucian's dialogue picks up Xanthus where Homer left off, running to the sea to try to cool himself off. The incompatibility of water and fire is also a topic in the dialogue of Proteus and Menelaus (4).

ΞΑΝΘΟΣ: Δέξαι με, ὦ θάλαττα, δεινὰ πεπονθότα καὶ κατάσβεσόν μου τὰ τραύματα.

ΘΑΛΑΤΤΑ: Τί τοῦτο, ὦ Ξάνθε; τίς σε κατέκαυσεν;

ΞΑΝΘΟΣ: Ὁ Ἥφαιστος. ἀλλ' ἀπηνθράκωμαι ὅλος ὁ κακοδαίμων καὶ ζέω.

ΘΑΛΑΤΤΑ: Διὰ τί δαί σοι καὶ ἐνέβαλε τὸ πῦρ;

ἀπανθρακόω: to burn to a cinder
δεινός, -ή, -όν: fearful, terrible, dire
δέχομαι: to take, accept, receive
ἐμβάλλω: to throw in, put in
ζέω: to boil, seethe
Ἥφαιστος, ὁ: Hephaestus
θάλαττα, ἡ: the sea

κακοδαίμων, -ον: ill-fated, ill-starred
κατακαίω: to burn down, burn completely
κατασβέννυμι: to extinguish
ὅλος, -η, -ον: whole, entire
πάσχω: to suffer
πῦρ, τό: fire
τραῦμα, -ατος, τό: a wound, hurt

δέξαι: aor. imper., "receive!"
πεπονθότα: perf. part. of πάσχω, "me *having suffered*"
κατάσβεσόν: aor. imper. of κατα-σβέννυμι, "extinguish!"
κατέκαυσεν: aor., "who *burnt* you?"
ἀπηνθράκωμαι: perf. of ἀπο-ανθρακόω, "I have been burnt"
ἐνέβαλε: aor., "why *did he throw on*?" + dat.
δαί: used to strengthen the interrogative, "why on earth?"

ΞΑΝΘΟΣ: Διὰ τὸν ταύτης υἱὸν τῆς Θέτιδος· ἐπεὶ γὰρ φονεύοντα τοὺς Φρύγας ἱκετεύσας οὐκ ἔπαυσα τῆς ὀργῆς, ἀλλ᾽ ὑπὸ τῶν νεκρῶν ἐνέφραττέ μοι τὸν ῥοῦν, ἐλεήσας τοὺς ἀθλίους ἐπῆλθον ἐπικλύσαι ἐθέλων, ὡς φοβηθεὶς ἀπόσχοιτο τῶν ἀνδρῶν. ἐνταῦθα ὁ Ἥφαιστος — ἔτυχε γὰρ πλησίον που ὤν — πᾶν ὅσον οἶμαι ἐν τῇ καμίνῳ πῦρ εἶχεν καὶ ὅσον ἐν τῇ Αἴτνῃ καὶ εἴ ποθι ἄλλοθι φέρων ἐπῆλθέ μοι, καὶ ἔκαυσε μὲν τὰς πτελέας μου

ἀθλίος, -α, -ον: miserable
Αἴτνη, ἡ: Mt. Aetna, site of a famous volcano
ἄλλοθι: elsewhere
ἀπέχω: to keep off or away from
ἐθέλω: to will, wish, purpose
ἐλεέω: to have pity on, show mercy upon
ἐμφράττω: to block up
ἐπέρχομαι: to go upon, attack
ἐπικλύζω: to overflow
Θέτις, Θέτιδος, ἡ: Thetis
ἱκετεύω: to beg
καίω: to light, kindle
κάμινος, ἡ: an oven, furnace, kiln

νεκρός, ὁ: a dead body, corpse
ὀργή, ἡ: wrath
παύω: to stop X (*acc.*) from Y (*gen.*)
πλησίον: nearby
ποθι: anywhere
πτελέα, ἡ: an elm
πῦρ, τό: fire
ῥόος, ὁ: a stream, flow, current
υἱός, ὁ: a son
φοβέω: to frighten
φονεύω: to murder, kill, slay
Φρύξ, -γος, ὁ: a Phrygian, a Trojan

υἱὸν τῆς Θέτιδος: "son of Thetis" i.e. Achilles
φονεύοντα: pr. part. after ἔπαυσα, "I didn't stop him *killing*"
ἱκετεύσας: aor. part. instr., "stop him *by having begged*"
τῆς ὀργῆς: gen. of sep., "stop him *from his anger*"
ὑπὸ τῶν νεκρῶν: "blocking *with the bodies*," using the agency expression
ἐνέφραττε: impf., "*he was blocking* my flow"
ἐλεήσας: aor. part., "having pitied"
ἐπῆλθον: aor., "I attacked"
ἐπικλύσαι: aor. inf. of ἐπικλύζω, complementing ἐθέλων, "wishing *to drown*."
ὡς ... ἀπόσχοιτο: aor. opt. of ἀπέχω in purp. cl., "so he would desist from" + gen.
φοβηθεὶς: ao part. instr., "by having been frightened"
ἔτυχε: aor., "he happened to" + part.
ὤν: pr. part. supplementing ἔτυχε, "happened *to be*"
πᾶν οἶμαι: parenth., "all the fire, I suppose,"
ὅσον ... εἶχεν: impf., "bringing *whatever fire he had*"
ἐπῆλθέ: aor., "he attacked"

καὶ μυρίκας, ὤπτησε δὲ καὶ τοὺς κακοδαίμονας ἰχθῦς καὶ τὰς ἐγχέλεις, αὐτὸν δὲ ἐμὲ ὑπερκαχλάσαι ποιήσας μικροῦ δεῖν ὅλον ξηρὸν εἴργασται. ὁρᾷς γοῦν ὅπως διάκειμαι ὑπὸ τῶν ἐγκαυμάτων.

ΘΑΛΑΤΤΑ: Θολερός, ὦ Ξάνθε, καὶ θερμός, ὡς εἰκός, τὸ αἷμα μὲν ἀπὸ τῶν νεκρῶν, ἡ θέρμη δέ, ὡς φής, ἀπὸ τοῦ πυρός: καὶ εἰκότως, ὦ Ξάνθε, ὃς ἐπὶ τὸν ἐμὸν υἱωνὸν ὥρμησας οὐκ αἰδεσθεὶς ὅτι Νηρηΐδος υἱὸς ἦν.

αἰδέομαι: to be ashamed to do
αἷμα, -ατος, τό: blood
διάκειμαι: to be in a certain state
ἔγκαυμα, -ατος, τό: a sore from burning
ἔγχελυς, -εως, ὁ: an eel
εἰκός: reasonable, likely, good
εἰκότως: reasonably, naturally
ἐργάζομαι: to work, to make
θέρμη, ἡ: a heat, feverish heat
θερμός, -ή, -όν: hot, warm
θολερός, -ά, -όν: muddy, foul, polluted
ἰχθῦς, ὁ: a fish

κακοδαίμων, -ον: fated, ill-starred, miserable
μικρός, -ά, -όν: small, little
μυρίκη, ἡ: a tamarisk
νεκρός, ὁ: a dead body, corpse
ξηρός, -ά, -όν: dry
ὀπτάω: to roast
ὁρμάω: to urge, rise up against
ποιέω: to make, to do
πῦρ, τό: fire
υἱωνός, ὁ: a grandson
ὑπερκαχλάζω: to run bubbling over

ὤπτησε: aor. of ὀπτάω, "he roasted"
ἔκαυσε: cf. *Iliad* 21.350: καίοντο πτελέαι τε καὶ ... μυρῖκαι
αὐτὸν δὲ ἐμὲ: "and me myself"
ἰχθῦς: cf. *Iliad* 21.353: τείροντ' ἐγχέλυες τε καὶ ἰχθύες
ὑπερκαχλάσαι: aor. act. inf. after ποιήσας, "having made me *to boil over*"
μικροῦ δεῖν: literally, "to lack little" i.e. almost
ὅλον ξηρὸν: acc. pred., "he made me almost *completely dry*"
εἴργασται: perf., "*he made* me dry"
ὅπως διάκειμαι: ind. quest. after ὁρᾷς, "you see *how I am affected*"
ὡς εἰκός: parenthetical, "so it seems"
εἰκότως: reasonably, i.e. "you deserved it"
ὃς ... ὥρμησας: aor., "(you) who assaulted"
αἰδεσθεὶς: aor. part. pass., "having not been ashamed"

ΞΑΝΘΟΣ: Οὐκ ἔδει οὖν ἐλεῆσαι γείτονας ὄντας τοὺς Φρύγας;

ΘΑΛΑΤΤΑ: Τὸν Ἥφαιστον δὲ οὐκ ἔδει ἐλεῆσαι Θέτιδος υἱὸν ὄντα τὸν Ἀχιλλέα;

Water, or the Fight of Achilles against Scamander and Simoeis. Auguste Couder, 1819. Louvre, Paris.

γείτων, -ονος, ὁ: a neighbor
ἐθέλω: to will, wish, purpose

ἐλεέω: to have pity on, shew mercy upon

οὐκ ἔδει οὖν: expecting a positive answer, "so was it not necessary to"? + inf.
ἐλεῆσαι: aor. inf., the subject is Xanthos himself, "(for me) to pity"
ὄντας: pr. part. causal, "*since they were* neighbors"
οὐκ ἔδει: "was it not necessary? + inf.
ὄντα: pr. part. causal, "*since he was* the son"

12. Doris and Thetis

The story of Perseus and Danae at the hands of Acrisus is the subject of this dialogue. Central to Lucian's version is the innocence of the child and the nobility of his mother, emphasized by the sympathy of the bystanders who witness the events, and their resolution to save the pair. Aeschylus composed a satyr play on the rescue of Perseus and Danae called the Netdrawers, referring to the rescue by fishermen.

ΔΩΡΙΣ: Τί δακρύεις, ὦ Θέτι;

ΘΕΤΙΣ: Καλλίστην, ὦ Δωρί, κόρην εἶδον ἐς κιβωτὸν ὑπὸ τοῦ πατρὸς ἐμβληθεῖσαν, αὐτήν τε καὶ βρέφος αὐτῆς ἀρτιγέννητον· ἐκέλευσεν δὲ ὁ πατὴρ τοὺς ναύτας ἀναλαβόντας τὸ κιβώτιον, ἐπειδὰν πολὺ τῆς γῆς ἀποσπάσωσιν, ἀφεῖναι ἐς τὴν θάλατταν, ὡς ἀπόλοιτο ἡ ἀθλία, καὶ αὐτὴ καὶ τὸ βρέφος.

ἄθλιος, -α, -ον: miserable
ἀναλαμβάνω: to take up, take into one's hands
ἀπόλλυμι: to destroy utterly, kill, slay
ἀποσπάω: to tear or drag away from
ἀρτιγέννητος, -ον: just born
ἀφίημι: to send forth, discharge
βρέφος, -εος, τό: a newborn
δακρύω: to weep, shed tears

ἐμβάλλω: to throw in, put in
ἐπειδάν: whenever (+ *subj.*)
θάλαττα, ἡ: the sea
Θέτις, Θέτιδος, ἡ: Thetis
κελεύω: to command
κιβώτιον, τό: a box
κόρη, ἡ: a maiden
ναύτης, -ου, ὁ: a sailor
πατήρ, πατρός, ὁ: a father

καλλίστην … κόρην: i.e. Danae, the daughter of Acrisius
κόρην … ἐμβληθεῖσαν: aor. part. pass. in ind. st. after εἶδον, "I saw *a girl thrown into*"
βρέφος: i.e. Perseus
ἀναλαβόντας: aor. part., "the sailors *who took up* the box"
ἐπειδὰν … ἀποσπάσωσιν: aor. subj. in gen. temp. cl., "after they drag it away from" + gen.
ἀφεῖναι: aor. inf. of ἀπο-ἵημι in ind. com. after ἐκέλευσεν, "ordered them *to cast it away*"
ὡς ἀπόλοιτο: aor. opt. in purp. cl., "so that they would die"
καὶ … καὶ: "both … and"

ΔΩΡΙΣ: Τίνος δὲ ἕνεκα, ὦ ἀδελφή; εἰπέ, εἴ τι ἔμαθες ἀκριβῶς ἅπαντα.

ΘΕΤΙΣ: Ὁ Ἀκρίσιος ὁ πατὴρ αὐτῆς καλλίστην οὖσαν ἐπαρθένευεν ἐς χαλκοῦν τινα θάλαμον ἐμβαλών· εἶτα, εἰ μὲν ἀληθὲς οὐκ ἔχω εἰπεῖν, φασὶ δ' οὖν τὸν Δία χρυσὸν γενόμενον ῥυῆναι διὰ τοῦ ὀρόφου ἐπ' αὐτήν, δεξαμένην δὲ ἐκείνην ἐς τὸν κόλπον καταρρέοντα τὸν θεὸν ἐγκύμονα γενέσθαι. τοῦτο αἰσθόμενος ὁ πατήρ, ἄγριός τις καὶ ζηλότυπος γέρων, ἠγανάκτησε καὶ ὑπό τινος μεμοιχεῦσθαι οἰηθεὶς αὐτὴν ἐμβάλλει ἐς τὴν κιβωτὸν ἄρτι τετοκυῖαν.

ἀγανακτέω: to feel irritation
ἄγριος, -α, -ον: cruel
ἀδελφή, ἡ: a sister
αἰσθάνομαι: to perceive
ἀκριβῶς: accurately
Ἀκρίσιος, ὁ: Acrisius
ἀληθής, -ές: unconcealed, true
ἄρτι: just, exactly
γέρων, -οντος, ὁ: an old man
δέχομαι: to take, accept, receive
ἐγκύμων, -ον: pregnant
ἐμβάλλω: to throw in, put in
ἕνεκα: on account of (+ gen.)
ἔχω: I am able (+ inf.)

ζηλότυπος, -ον: jealous
θάλαμος, ὁ: an inner room or chamber
καταρρέω: to flow down
κιβωτός, ἡ: a wooden box, chest, coffer
κόλπος, ὁ: a bosom
μανθάνω: to learn
μοιχεύω: to commit adultery with
οἴμαι: to suppose
ὄροφος, ὁ: a roof
παρθενεύω: to bring up as a maid
ῥέω: to flow, run, stream, gush
τίκτω: to give birth
χάλκεος, -ῆ, -οῦν: of copper or bronze
χρυσός, ὁ: gold

καλλίστην οὖσαν: pr. part. causal, "because she was very beautiful"
ἐμβαλών: aor. part., "having her thrown into"
εἰ μὲν ἀληθὲς (sc. ἐστι): ind. quest. after εἰπεῖν, "to say *whether it is true*"
γενόμενον: aor. part., "Zeus *having become* gold"
ῥυῆναι: aor. inf. pass. in ind. st. after φασὶ, "they say *that Zeus flowed*"
δεξαμένην: aor. mid. part., "(her) *having received* the god"
καταρρέοντα: pr. part. agreeing with τὸν θεὸν, "the god *flowing down*"
γενέσθαι: aor. inf. in ind. st. after φασὶ, "*that she became* pregnant"
αἰσθόμενος: aor. part., "having perceived"
ἠγανάκτησε: aor. inceptive, "he became angry"
μεμοιχεῦσθαι: perf. inf. pass. after οἰηθεὶς, "having supposed her *to have committed adultery* at the hands of someone"
οἰηθεὶς: aor. part. pass., "having supposed"
ἄρτι τετοκυῖαν: perf. part. of τίκτω, "just after she had given birth"

ΔΩΡΙΣ: Ἡ δὲ τί ἔπραττεν, ὦ Θέτι, ὁπότε καθίετο;

ΘΕΤΙΣ: Ὑπὲρ αὑτῆς μὲν ἐσίγα, ὦ Δωρί, καὶ ἔφερε τὴν καταδίκην. τὸ βρέφος δὲ παρῃτεῖτο μὴ ἀποθανεῖν δακρύουσα καὶ τῷ πάππῳ δεικνύουσα αὐτό, κάλλιστον ὄν· τὸ δὲ ὑπ' ἀγνοίας τῶν κακῶν ὑπεμειδία πρὸς τὴν θάλατταν. ὑποπίμπλαμαι αὖθις τοὺς ὀφθαλμοὺς δακρύων μνημονεύσασα αὐτῶν.

ΔΩΡΙΣ: Κἀμὲ δακρῦσαι ἐποίησας. ἀλλ' ἤδη τεθνᾶσιν;

ἄγνοια, ἡ: a want of perception, ignorance of (+ *gen.*)
ἀποθνῄσκω: to die
αὖθις: back, back again
βρέφος, -εος, τό: a newborn
δακρύω: to weep, shed tears
δείκνυμι: to show to (+ *dat.*)
Δωρίς, -ίδος, ἡ: Doris
θάλαττα, ἡ: the sea
Θέτις, Θέτιδος, ἡ: Thetis
θνῄσκω: to die
καθίημι: to send down, let fall
κακός, -ή, -όν: bad, trouble, evil

καταδίκη, ἡ: a sentence
μνημονεύω: to call to mind, remember
ὁπότε: when
ὀφθαλμός, ὁ: an eye
πάππος, ὁ: a grandfather
παραιτέομαι: to beg from
ποιέω: to make
πράττω: to do
σιγάω: to be silent or still, to keep silence
ὑπομειδιάω: to smile a little or gently
ὑποπίμπλημι: to fill X (*acc.*) with Y (*gen.*)
φέρω: to bear

ἡ δὲ: "but she" i.e. Danae
ὁπότε καθίετο: impf. of κατα-ἵημι, "when he was putting her down"
ἐσίγα: impf., "she was silent"
παρῃτεῖτο: impf. of παρα-αἰτέομαι, "she kept on begging"
μὴ ἀποθανεῖν: aor. inf. in ind. com., "begging *not to kill*"
δακρύουσα: pr. part., "shedding tears"
δεικνύουσα: pr. part., "showing it to" + dat.
τὸ δὲ: "but that one," i.e. the baby
ὑπεμειδία: impf., "was smiling"
δακρύων: pr. part. instrumental, "by crying"
μνημονεύσασα: aor. part., "remembering" + gen.
κἀμὲ: = καί + ἐμέ
δακρῦσαι: inf. after ἐποίησας, "you made me *to cry*"
τεθνᾶσιν: perf. of θνῄσκω, "are they already dead?"

ΘΕΤΙΣ: Οὐδαμῶς· νήχεται γὰρ ἔτι ἡ κιβωτὸς ἀμφὶ τὴν Σέριφον ζῶντας αὐτοὺς φυλάττουσα.

ΔΩΡΙΣ: Τί οὖν οὐχὶ σῴζομεν αὐτὴν τοῖς ἁλιεῦσι τούτοις ἐμβαλοῦσαι ἐς τὰ δίκτυα τοῖς Σεριφίοις; οἱ δὲ ἀνασπάσαντες σώσουσι δῆλον ὅτι.

ΘΕΤΙΣ: Εὖ λέγεις, οὕτω ποιῶμεν· μὴ γὰρ ἀπολέσθω μήτε αὐτὴ μήτε τὸ παιδίον οὕτως ὂν καλόν.

ἁλιεύς, εως, ὁ: a fisherman
ἀμφί: around
ἀνασπάω: to draw up
ἀπόλλυμι: to destroy utterly, kill, slay
δίκτυον, τό: a casting-net, a net
ἐμβάλλω: to throw in, put in
ζάω: to live
κιβωτός, ἡ: a wooden box, chest, coffer
νήχω: to swim, to float
ποιέω: to make
Σερίφιος, -η, -ον: Seriphian
Σέριφος, ἡ: Seriphos
σῴζω: to save
φυλάττω: to keep watch and ward, keep guard

Σέριφον: Seriphos, the island to which Danae and Perseus drifted
σῴζομεν: deliberative question, where a subjunctive is more usual, "why don't we save her?"
ἁλιεῦσι ... Σεριφίοις: dat. of possession, "nets *of the Seriphian fishermen*"
ἐμβαλοῦσαι: aor. part. instr., "we *by having placed* them"
οἱ δὲ: "and they" i.e. the fishermen
ἀνασπάσαντες: aor. part., "having drawn up"
δῆλον (sc. ἐστι) ὅτι: "it is clear that" i.e. clearly
ποιῶμεν: pr. subj. jussive, "let us do it"
μὴ ἀπολέσθω: aor. imper. 3 s., "let her not die"
μήτε ... μήτε: "neither ... nor," reinforcing the negative
ὂν: pr. part. causal, "*since he is* beautiful"

13. Enipeus and Poseidon

This episode is based on Odyssey 9, 235-59, where the story of Tyro is told. Poseidon likened himself to the river god Enipeus, with whom Tyro was enamored, and slept with her. Lucian's version presents Poseidon as mocking Enipeus for being too haughty toward Tyro, and thus making it possible for Poseidon to enjoy her instead. Epineus' prominence in this dialogue is a contrast to his virtual absence in the Odyssey version.

ΕΝΙΠΕΥΣ: Οὐ καλὰ ταῦτα, ὦ Πόσειδον: εἰρήσεται γὰρ τἀληθές: ὑπελθών μου τὴν ἐρωμένην εἰκασθεὶς ἐμοὶ διεκόρευσας τὴν παῖδα: ἡ δὲ ᾤετο ὑπ' ἐμοῦ ταῦτα πεπονθέναι καὶ διὰ τοῦτο παρεῖχεν ἑαυτήν.

ΠΟΣΕΙΔΩΝ: Σὺ γάρ, ὦ Ἐνιπεῦ, ὑπεροπτικὸς ἦσθα καὶ βραδύς, ὃς κόρης οὕτω καλῆς φοιτώσης ὁσημέραι παρὰ σέ, ἀπολλυμένης ὑπὸ τοῦ ἔρωτος, ὑπερεώρας καὶ

ἀληθής, -ές: unconcealed, true
ἀπόλλυμι: to destroy utterly, kill
βραδύς, -εῖα, -ύ: slow
διακορεύω: to deflower
εἰκάζω: to make like, represent by a likeness
ἐράω: to love
καλός, -ή, -όν: beautiful
κόρη, ἡ: a maiden
οἶμαι: to suppose, think

ὁσημέραι: (*adv.*) every day
παῖς, παιδός, ἡ: a child
παρέχω: to provide, submit
πάσχω: to suffer, experience
ὑπεροπτικός, -ή, -όν: contemptuous, disdainful
ὑπεροράω: to look over, look down upon
ὑπέρχομαι: to go under, enter, entrap
φοιτάω: to go to and fro

εἰρήσεται: fut. perf. of λέγω, "the truth *will be told*"
ὑπελθών: aor. part. of ὑπο-ἔρχομαι, "having entrapped"
τὴν ἐρωμένην: pr. part. pass. acc., "my beloved"
εἰκασθεὶς: aor. part. pass., "having likened yourself to" + dat.
διεκόρευσας: aor., "you deflowered the child"
ἡ δὲ: "but she"
ᾤετο: impf., "she was supposing" + inf.
πεπονθέναι: perf. inf. of πάσχω, in ind. st. after ᾤετο, "supposing *that she suffered*"
κόρης ... φοιτώσης: pr. part. in gen. abs., "*a pretty girl coming* to you"
ἀπολλυμένης: pr. part. also in gen. abs., "a girl *dying* from love"
ὑπὸ τοῦ ἔρωτος: agency expression, "dying *from love*"
ὑπερεώρας: aor., "you (who) despised her"

ἔχαιρες λυπῶν αὐτήν, ἡ δὲ περὶ τὰς ὄχθας ἀλύουσα καὶ ἐπεμβαίνουσα καὶ λουομένη ἐνίοτε ηὔχετό σοι ἐντυχεῖν, σὺ δὲ ἐθρύπτου πρὸς αὐτήν.

ΕΝΙΠΕΥΣ: Τί οὖν; διὰ τοῦτο ἐχρῆν σε προαρπάσαι τὸν ἔρωτα καὶ καθυποκρίνασθαι Ἐνιπέα ἀντὶ Ποσειδῶνος εἶναι καὶ κατασοφίσασθαι τὴν Τυρὼ ἀφελῆ κόρην οὖσαν;

ΠΟΣΕΙΔΩΝ: Ὀψὲ ζηλοτυπεῖς, ὦ Ἐνιπεῦ, ὑπερόπτης πρότερον ὤν· ἡ Τυρὼ δὲ οὐδὲ δεινὸν πέπονθεν οἰομένη ὑπὸ σοῦ διακεκορεῦσθαι.

ἀλύω: to be distraught
ἀντί: instead of (+ *gen.*)
ἀφελής, -ές: simple, guileless
δεινός, -ή, -όν: fearful, terrible
ἐνίοτε: sometimes
Ἐνιπεύς, ὁ: Enipeus, a river-god
ἐντυγχάνω: to light upon, encounter (+ *dat.*)
ἐπεμβαίνω: to step or tread upon
εὔχομαι: to pray, make a vow
ζηλοτυπέω: to be jealous of, to emulate, rival
θρύπτομαι: to be coy, to put on airs
καθυποκρίνομαι: to pretend to (+ *inf.*)
κατασοφίζομαι: to outwit

κόρη, ἡ: a maiden
λούω: to wash
λυπέω: to cause pain
οἶμαι: to suppose, think
ὄχθη, ἡ: a river bank
ὀψέ: late
πάσχω: to suffer
προαρπάζω: to snatch away before
πρότερον: previously
Τυρώ, ἡ: Tyro, mother of Pelias and Neleus
ὑπερόπτης, -ου, ὁ: a disdainer or dispiser
χαίρω: to rejoice (+ *part.*)
χρή: it is fated, necessary

λυπῶν: pr. part. suppl. after ἔχαιρες, "you rejoiced *causing her to grieve*"
ἡ δὲ: "but she" i.e. the girl
ἐπεμβαίνουσα: pr. part. of ἐπι-εν-βαίνω, "stepping upon"
ηὔχετό: impf. of εὔχομαι, "she kept praying" + inf.
ἐντυχεῖν: aor. inf., "praying *to encounter*"
ἐθρύπτου: impf., "you were giving airs towards her"
τί οὖν: "so what?"
προαρπάσαι: aor. inf. after ἐχρῆν, "was it necessary *to snatch away* her love?"
καθυποκρίνασθαι: aor. inf. of κατα-ὑπο-κρίνομαι after ἐχρῆν, "necessary *to pretend to* be"
κατασοφίσασθαι: aor. inf. also after ἐχρῆν, "and to outwit"
ἀφελῆ κόρην: acc. pred., "being *a simple maiden*"
πέπονθεν: perf., "Tyro *has suffered*"
οἰομένη: pr. part. instr., "suffered *by thinking*"
ὑπὸ σοῦ: agency, "by you"
διακεκορεῦσθαι: perf. inf. pass. in ind. st., "thinking *to have been deflowered*"

ΕΝΙΠΕΥΣ: Οὐ μὲν οὖν· ἔφησθα γὰρ ἀπιὼν ὅτι Ποσειδῶν ἦσθα. ὃ καὶ μάλιστα ἐλύπησεν αὐτήν· καὶ ἐγὼ τοῦτο ἠδίκημαι, ὅτι τὰ ἐμὰ σὺ ηὐφραίνου τότε καὶ περιστήσας πορφύρεόν τι κῦμα, ὅπερ ὑμᾶς συνέκρυπτεν ἅμα, συνῆσθα τῇ παιδὶ ἀντ' ἐμοῦ.

ΠΟΣΕΙΔΩΝ: Ναί· σὺ γὰρ οὐκ ἤθελες, ὦ Ἐνιπεῦ.

ἀδικέω: to do wrong
ἀπέρχομαι: to go away
ἐθέλω: to will, wish, purpose
εὐφραίνομαι: to enjoy
κῦμα, -ατος, τό: a wave
λυπέω: to pain, distress

παῖς, παιδός, ὁ: a child, girl
περιίστημι: to place round
πορφύρεος: dark gleaming, dark
σύνειμι: to be with, to have intercourse with
συνκρύπτω: to hide together
τότε: at that time, then

οὐ μὲν οὖν: "no, not at all"
ἔφησθα: aor., "you said"
ἀπιών: pr. part., "as you were leaving"
ὅτι ... ἦσθα: ind. st., "*that you were* Poseidon"
ἠδίκημαι: perf. pass. of ἀδικέω, "I have been wronged"
ὅτι ... ηὐφραίνου: impf. of εὐφραίνω, "because you enjoyed"
περιστήσας: aor. part. trans. of περι-ίστημι, "having placed around"
συνῆσθα: impf. of σύν-ειμι, "you were having intercourse with" + dat.
ἤθελες: impf. of ἐθέλω, "you were not wishing"

14. Triton and the Nereids

Another episode from the life of Perseus (cf. #12) is related by sea creatures, this time his slaying of the sea monster and marriage to Andromeda. The sea monster had been sent by the sea nymphs as a punishment for the haughtiness of Andromeda's mother, Cassiopeia. Although initially miffed that Perseus has not turned out to be grateful for his earlier rescue, the nymphs eventually come around to celebrating the wedding of Andromeda and Perseus. This material was the subject of plays by Euripides and Sophocles and is celebrated in painting and ekphrasis, such as Achilles Tatius' Leucippe, 3. 6-7.

ΤΡΙΤΩΝ: Τὸ κῆτος ὑμῶν, ὦ Νηρηΐδες, ὃ ἐπὶ τὴν τοῦ Κηφέως θυγατέρα τὴν Ἀνδρομέδαν ἐπέμψατε, οὔτε τὴν παῖδα ἠδίκησεν, ὡς οἴεσθε, καὶ αὐτὸ ἤδη τέθνηκεν.

ΝΗΡΕΙΔΕΣ: Ὑπὸ τίνος, ὦ Τρίτων; ἢ ὁ Κηφεὺς καθάπερ δέλεαρ προθεὶς τὴν κόρην ἀπέκτεινεν ἐπιών, λοχήσας μετὰ πολλῆς δυνάμεως;

ἀδικέω: to do wrong, harm
Ἀνδρομέδα, ἡ: Andromeda
ἀποκτείνω: to kill, slay
δέλεαρ, -ατος, τό: a bait
δύναμις, -εως, ἡ: a power, force (of men)
ἐπέρχομαι: to go against, attack
θνῄσκω: to die
θυγάτηρ, -έρος, ἡ: a daughter
καθάπερ: just like
κῆτος, -εος, τό: a sea monster

Κηφεύς, ὁ: Cepheus
κόρη, ἡ: a maiden
λοχάω: to lie in wait for, to watch, waylay, entrap
Νηρηΐς, ἡ: a Nereid
οἶμαι: to suppose
παῖς, παιδός, ὁ: a child
πέμπω: to send
προτίθημι: to place or set before, set out
Τρίτων, -ωνος, ὁ: Triton

ὃ ... ἐπέμψατε: aor., "which you sent"
ἠδίκησεν: aor., "did not harm"
ὡς οἴεσθε: parenth., "as you suppose"
αὐτὸ: i.e. the monster
τέθνηκεν: perf. of θνῄσκω, "is dead"
προθεὶς: aor. part. of προτίθημι, "*having set out* the girl"
ἀπέκτεινεν: aor., "did he kill him?"
ἐπιών: pr. part. instr. of ἐπι-έρχομαι, "by attacking"
λοχήσας: aor. part., "having lain in wait"

ΤΡΙΤΩΝ: Οὔκ· ἀλλὰ ἴστε, οἶμαι, ὦ Ἰφιάνασσα, τὸν Περσέα, τὸ τῆς Δανάης παιδίον, ὃ μετὰ τῆς μητρὸς ἐν τῇ κιβωτῷ ἐμβληθὲν εἰς τὴν θάλατταν ὑπὸ τοῦ μητροπάτορος ἐσώσατε οἰκτείρασαι αὐτούς.

ΙΦΙΑΝΑΣΣΑ: Οἶδα ὃν λέγεις· εἰκὸς δὲ ἤδη νεανίαν εἶναι καὶ μάλα γενναῖόν τε καὶ καλὸν ἰδεῖν.

ΤΡΙΤΩΝ: Οὗτος ἀπέκτεινεν τὸ κῆτος.

ΙΦΙΑΝΑΣΣΑ: Διὰ τί, ὦ Τρίτων; οὐ γὰρ δὴ σῶστρα ἡμῖν τοιαῦτα ἐκτίνειν αὐτὸν ἐχρῆν.

ἀποκτείνω: to kill, slay
γενναῖος, -α, -ον: suitable to one's birth
Δανάη, ἡ: Danae
ἐκτίνω: to pay off, pay in full
ἐμβάλλω: to throw in, put in
θάλαττα, ἡ: the sea
Ἰφιάνασσα, ἡ: Iphianassa, one of the Nereids
κιβωτός, ἡ: a wooden box, chest, coffer
μήτηρ, μητρός, ἡ: a mother
μητροπάτωρ, -ορος, ὁ: one's mother's father
νεανίας, -ου, ὁ: a young man
οἶδα: to know
οἰκτείρω: to pity
παιδίον, τό: a child
Περσεύς, ὁ: Perseus
σῴζω: to keep, save
σῶστρα, τά: a thankoffering for deliverance
χρή: it is fated, necessary

ἐμβληθὲν: aor. pass. part., "having been thrown in"
μητροπάτορος: one's mother's father, i.e. Acrisius
ἐσώσατε: aor., "you saved him"
οἰκτείρασαι: aor. part., "you *having taken pity on* him"
εἰκὸς (sc. ἐστι): "and now it is *likely*"
νεανίαν εἶναι: ind. st. after εἰκὸς, "likely *that he is a young man*"
ἰδεῖν: aor. inf. epex., "handome *to see*"
ἀπέκτεινεν: aor., "this one *killed*"
ἐκτίνειν: pr. inf. after οὐ ἐχρῆν, "it was not necessary for him *to pay us back*"

Lucian

ΤΡΙΤΩΝ: Ἐγὼ ὑμῖν φράσω τὸ πᾶν ὡς ἐγένετο· ἐστάλη μὲν οὗτος ἐπὶ τὰς Γοργόνας ἆθλόν τινα τοῦτον τῷ βασιλεῖ ἐπιτελῶν, ἐπεὶ δὲ ἀφίκετο εἰς τὴν Λιβύην —

ΙΦΙΑΝΑΣΣΑ: Πῶς, ὦ Τρίτων; μόνος; ἢ καὶ ἄλλους συμμάχους ἦγεν; ἄλλως γὰρ δύσπορος ἡ ὁδός.

ΤΡΙΤΩΝ: Διὰ τοῦ ἀέρος· ὑπόπτερον γὰρ αὐτὸν ἡ Ἀθηνᾶ ἔθηκεν. ἐπεὶ δ' οὖν ἦκεν ὅπου διῃτῶντο, αἱ μὲν ἐκάθευδον, οἶμαι, ὁ δὲ ἀποτεμὼν τῆς Μεδούσης τὴν κεφαλὴν ᾤχετο ἀποπτάμενος.

ἄγω: to lead or carry
ἀήρ, ἀέρος, ὁ: air
Ἀθηνᾶ, ἡ: Athena
ἆθλον, τό: a task, labor
ἄλλως: otherwise
ἀποπέτομαι: to fly off or away
ἀποτέμνω: to cut off, sever
ἀφικνέομαι: to come to
βασιλεύς, -έως, ὁ: a king, chief
Γοργώ, -ονος, ἡ: the Gorgon
διαιτάω: to lead one's life, live
δύσπορος, -ον: hard to pass, scarce passable
ἐπιτελέω: to complete, finish, accomplish
ἥκω: to have come, be present, be here

καθεύδω: to sleep
κεφαλή, ἡ: a head
Λιβύη, ἡ: Libya
Μεδούση, -ης, ἡ: Medusa, the Gorgon
μόνος, -η, -ον: alone
ὁδός, ἡ: a way, path
οἶμαι: to suppose, think
οἴχομαι: to be gone, depart
στέλλω: to send, equip
σύμμαχος, -ου, ὁ: an ally
τίθημι: to set, put, establish
ὑπόπτερος, -ον: winged
φράζω: to point out, show

ὡς ἐγένετο: aor. in ind. st., "tell *how it happened*"
ἐστάλη: aor. pass. of στέλλω, "he was sent against"
τῷ βασιλεῖ: dat., "for the king," Polydectes was the king of Seriphos, who sent Perseus on this mission to get rid of him
ἐπιτελῶν: fut. part. showing purpose, "*in order to complete* the task"
ἀφίκετο: aor. of ἀπο-ικνέομαι, "after *he arrived*"
ἦγεν: impf., "was he leading?"
ὑπόπτερον: acc. predicate, "she made him *winged*"
ἔθηκεν: aor. of τίθημι, "she established him"
ὅπου διῃτῶντο: impf. in ind. ques., "where they were living"
αἱ μὲν … ὁ δὲ: "while they… but he"
ἀποτεμὼν: aor. part., "having cut off"
ἀποπτάμενος: aor. part. of ἀποπέτομαι, "having flown off"

ΙΦΙΑΝΑΣΣΑ: Πῶς ἰδών; ἀθέατοι γάρ εἰσιν· ἢ ὃς ἂν ἴδῃ, οὐκ ἄν τι ἄλλο μετὰ ταύτας ἴδοι.

ΤΡΙΤΩΝ: Ἡ Ἀθηνᾶ τὴν ἀσπίδα προφαίνουσα — τοιαῦτα γὰρ ἤκουσα διηγουμένου αὐτοῦ πρὸς τὴν Ἀνδρομέδαν καὶ πρὸς τὸν Κηφέα ὕστερον — ἡ Ἀθηνᾶ δὴ ἐπὶ τῆς ἀσπίδος ἀποστιλβούσης ὥσπερ ἐπὶ κατόπτρου παρέσχεν αὐτῷ ἰδεῖν τὴν εἰκόνα τῆς Μεδούσης· εἶτα λαβόμενος τῇ λαιᾷ τῆς κόμης, ἐνορῶν δ' ἐς τὴν εἰκόνα, τῇ δεξιᾷ τὴν ἅρπην ἔχων, ἀπέτεμε τὴν κεφαλὴν αὐτῆς, καὶ πρὶν ἀνεγρέσθαι τὰς ἀδελφὰς ἀνέπτατο. ἐπεὶ δὲ

ἀδελφή, ἡ: a sister
ἀθέατος, -ον: unseen, invisible
Ἀθηνᾶ, ἡ: Athena
ἀκούω: to hear X (acc.) from Y (gen.)
ἀναπέτομαι: to fly up, fly away
Ἀνδρομέδα, ἡ: Andromeda
ἀνεγείρω: to wake up, rouse
ἀποστίλβω: to be bright, gleam
ἀποτέμνω: to cut off, sever
ἅρπη, ἡ: a scimitar, a kind of weapon
ἀσπίς, -ίδος, ἡ: a round shield
δεξιά, ἡ: a right hand
διηγέομαι: to set out in detail, describe in full

εἰκών, -όνος, ἡ: a likeness, image
ἐνοράω: to see, observe
κάτοπτρον, τό: a mirror
κεφαλή, ἡ: a head
Κηφεύς, έως, ὁ: Cepheus, father of Andromeda
κόμη, ἡ: hair
λαιός, -ά, -όν: on the left
λαμβάνω: to take
παρέχω: to provide, to allow (+ inf.)
πρίν: before (+ inf.)
προφαίνω: to show forth
ὕστερον: later

ὃς ἂν ἴδῃ: aor. subj. of εἶδον in gen. rel. clause, "whoever sees"
ἄν ... ἴδοι: aor. opt. pot. of εἶδον, "*he would not see* anything else"
προφαίνουσα: pr. part., "*showing forth* her shield"
αὐτοῦ διηγουμένου: pr. part. gen. of source after ἤκουσα, "I heard *him narrating* these things"
ἡ Ἀθηνᾶ δή: the subject is repeated after the parenthetical comment
ἀποστιλβούσης: pr. part. agreeing with ἀσπίδος, "the shield *being bright*"
παρέσχεν: aor., "she allowed" + inf.
ἰδεῖν: aor. inf. complementing παρέσχεν, "allowed him *to see*"
λαβόμενος: aor. part., "having seized" + gen.
τῇ λαιᾷ ... τῇ δεξιᾷ: "with the left hand…with the right hand"
ἀπέτεμε: aor., "he cut off"
πρὶν ἀνεγρέσθαι: aor. inf., "before the sisters *woke up*"
ἀνέπτατο: aor. of ἀνα-πέτομαι, "he flew away"

κατὰ τὴν παράλιον ταύτην Αἰθιοπίαν ἐγένετο, ἤδη
πρόσγειος πετόμενος, ὁρᾷ τὴν Ἀνδρομέδαν προκειμένην
ἐπί τινος πέτρας προβλῆτος προσπεπατταλευμένην,
καλλίστην, ὦ θεοί, καθειμένην τὰς κόμας, ἡμίγυμνον
πολὺ ἔνερθε τῶν μαστῶν· καὶ τὸ μὲν πρῶτον οἰκτείρας
τὴν τύχην αὐτῆς ἀνηρώτα τὴν αἰτίαν τῆς καταδίκης,
κατὰ μικρὸν δὲ ἁλοὺς ἔρωτι — ἐχρῆν γὰρ σεσῶσθαι
τὴν παῖδα — βοηθεῖν διέγνω· καὶ ἐπειδὴ τὸ κῆτος
ἐπῄει μάλα φοβερὸν ὡς καταπιόμενον τὴν Ἀνδρομέδαν,

Αἰθιοπίος, -α, ον: Ethipoian
αἰτία, ἡ: a charge, cause
ἁλίσκομαι: to be taken, conquered, captured
ἀνερωτάω: to ask or inquire of, question
βοηθέω: to help
διαγινώσκω: to distinguish, discern
ἔνερθε: beneath (+ *gen.*)
ἐπέρχομαι: to approach
ἔρως, -ωτος, ὁ: love
ἡμίγυμνος, -ον: half-naked
καθίημι: to send down, let fall
καταδίκη, ἡ: a judgment given against one
καταπίνω: to gulp or swallow down
κῆτος, τό: a monster

κόμη, ἡ: hair
μαστός, ὁ: a breast
μικρός, -ά, -όν: small, little
οἰκτείρω: to pity
ὁράω: to see
παράλιη, ἡ: a shore
πέτομαι: to fly
πέτρα, ἡ: a rock, a ledge
προβλής, -ῆτος: forestretching, jutting
πρόκειμαι: to be set before one
πρόσγειος, -ον: near the earth, near the ground
προσπατταλεύω: to nail fast to, to fasten
τύχη, ἡ: fate
φοβερός, -ά, -όν: fearful

προκειμένην: perf. part., "Andromeda *having been set before*"
προσπεπατταλευμένην: perf. part. pass., "her having been fastened"
καθειμένην: perf. part. mid. of κατα-ίημι, "*having let down* her hair"
τῶν μαστῶν: gen. after ἔνερθε, "below her breasts"
οἰκτείρας: aor. part., "at first *having pitied*"
ἀνηρώτα: impf. of ἀνα-ερωτάω, "he asked"
κατὰ μικρὸν: "little by little"
ἁλοὺς: aor. part. of ἁλίσκομαι, "having been captured"
σεσῶσθαι: perf. inf. complementing ἐχρῆν, "it was necessary for the girl *to be saved*"
διέγνω: aor. of διαγινώσκω, "he decided" + inf.
ἐπειδὴ ... ἐπῄει: impf., "when the sea-monster was approaching"
ὡς καταπιόμενον: fut. part. mid. expressing purpose, "in order to gulp down"

Dialogues of the Sea Gods

ὑπεραιωρηθεὶς ὁ νεανίσκος πρόκωπον ἔχων τὴν ἅρπην τῇ μὲν καθικνεῖται, τῇ δὲ προδεικνὺς τὴν Γοργόνα λίθον ἐποίει αὐτό, τὸ δὲ τέθνηκεν ὁμοῦ καὶ πέπηγεν αὐτοῦ τὰ πολλά, ὅσα εἶδε τὴν Μέδουσαν· ὁ δὲ λύσας τὰ δεσμὰ τῆς παρθένου, ὑποσχὼν τὴν χεῖρα ὑπεδέξατο ἀκροποδητὶ κατιοῦσαν ἐκ τῆς πέτρας ὀλισθηρᾶς οὔσης, καὶ νῦν γαμεῖ ἐν τοῦ Κηφέως καὶ ἀπάξει αὐτὴν εἰς Ἄργος, ὥστε ἀντὶ θανάτου γάμον οὐ τὸν τυχόντα εὕρετο.

ἀκροποδητί: on tiptoe
ἀντί: instead of (+ *gen.*)
ἀπάγω: to lead away, carry off
ἅρπη, ἡ: a scimitar
γαμέω: to marry
γάμος, ὁ: a wedding
δεσμά, τά: fetters
εὑρίσκω: to find
θάνατος, ὁ: death
θνῄσκω: to die
καθικνέομαι: to come down to
κατέρχομαι: to go, to come down
λίθος ὁ: a stone
λύω: to loose

νεανίσκος, ὁ: a youth
ὀλισθηρός, -ά, -όν: slippery
ὁμοῦ: at the same time
παρθένος, -ου, ἡ: a maid, maiden, virgin, girl
πέτρα, ἡ: a rock
πήγνυμι: to make solid
ποιέω: to make
προδείκνυμι: to display forth
πρόκωπος, -ον: grasped by the hilt, drawn
τυγχάνω: to happen upon
ὑπεραιωρέω: to suspend above
ὑπέχω: to hold or put under
ὑποδέχομαι: to receive beneath
χείρ, χειρός, ἡ: a hand

ὑπεραιωρηθεὶς: aor. pass. part., "having been suspended"
ἔχων τῇ μὲν: "while having in one (hand)"
προδεικνὺς τῇ δὲ: "*in the other hand showing* the Gorgon"
λίθον: acc. pred., "he made it (i.e. the monster) *stone*"
τὸ δὲ: "but it" i.e. the monster
πέπηγεν: perf., "most of it *became solid*"
ὅσα εἶδε: "whatever part he saw"
λύσας: aor. part., "but he *having loosened*"
ὑποσχὼν: aor. part., "*having supported* her"
ὑπεδέξατο: aor., "he received"
κατιοῦσαν: pr. part. acc., "her *coming down* from the rock"
ὀλισθηρᾶς: gen. pred., "the rock being *slippery*"
ἐν (οἴκῳ) τοῦ Κηφέως: gen. place where, "in Cepheus' palace"
ἀπάξει: fut., "he will lead"
ὥστε ... εὕρετο: aor. in res. cl., "so that ...she has found"
οὐ τὸν τυχόντα: aor. part. acc., "*the not happened (upon)* marriage" i.e. not by chance, not usual

69

ΙΦΙΑΝΑΣΣΑ: Ἐγὼ μὲν οὐ πάνυ τῷ γεγονότι ἄχθομαι· τί γὰρ ἡ παῖς ἠδίκει ἡμᾶς, εἰ ἡ μήτηρ, ἐμεγαλαυχεῖτο καὶ ἠξίου καλλίων εἶναι;

ΔΩΡΙΣ: Ὅτι οὕτως ἂν ἤλγησεν ἐπὶ τῇ θυγατρὶ μήτηρ γε οὖσα.

ΙΦΙΑΝΑΣΣΑ: Μηκέτι μεμνώμεθα, ὦ Δωρί, ἐκείνων, εἴ τι βάρβαρος γυνὴ ὑπὲρ τὴν ἀξίαν ἐλάλησεν· ἱκανὴν γὰρ ἡμῖν τιμωρίαν ἔδωκε φοβηθεῖσα ἐπὶ τῇ παιδί. χαίρωμεν οὖν τῷ γάμῳ.

ἀδικέω: to do wrong
ἀλγέω: to feel bodily pain, suffer
ἀξία, ἡ: worth, value
ἀξιόω: to think worthy of
ἄχθομαι: to be grieved
βάρβαρος, -ον: barbarous
γάμος, ὁ: a wedding, marriage
γυνή, γυναικός, ἡ: a woman
δίδωμι: to give
θυγάτηρ: a daughter
ἱκανός, -η, -ον: sufficient
καλλίων, καλλίον: more beautiful
λαλέω: to talk
μεγαλαυχέω: to boast highly, talk big
μήτηρ, μητρός, ἡ: a mother
μιμνήσκω: to remind, put
παῖς, παιδός, ὁ: a child
τιμωρία, ἡ: retribution
φοβέω: to frighten
χαίρω: to rejoice, be glad, be delighted

τῷ γεγονότι: perf. part. dat. of γίνομαι, after ἄχθομαι, "grieved at *what has happened*"
τί ... ἠδίκει: impf., "*why was she harming* us?"
ἠξίου: impf. of ἀξιόω, "*if she was claiming*" + inf.
ὅτι οὕτως: "because in this way," i.e. if the daughter had been harmed
ἂν ἤλγησεν: aor. in past contrafactual, "because *she (the mother) would have suffered*"
οὖσα: pr. part. causal, "*since she is* her mother"
μηκέτι μεμνώμεθα: perf. subj. jussive, "let us no longer remember" + gen.
ἐλάλησεν: aor., "if a barbarian woman *talked*"
τιμωρίαν ἔδωκε: aor., "she gave penalty"
φοβηθεῖσα: aor. pass. part instr., "by being frightened"
χαίρωμεν: pr. subj. jussive, "let us rejoice in" + dat.

15. Zephyrus and Notus

Zephyrus reports to Notus the abduction of Europa by Zeus in the form of a bull, and his travel to Crete with the girl on his back. The story is told in an aetiological poem by Moschus and is the subject of a famous ekphrasis in the opening pages of Achilles Tatius' Leucippe. These two winds also report the story of Io in #7 above.

ΖΕΦΥΡΟΣ: Οὐ πώποτε πομπὴν ἐγὼ μεγαλοπρεπεστέραν εἶδον ἐν τῇ θαλάττῃ, ἀφ' οὗ γέ εἰμι καὶ πνέω. σὺ δὲ οὐκ εἶδες, ὦ Νότε;

ΝΟΤΟΣ: Τίνα ταύτην λέγεις, ὦ Ζέφυρε, τὴν πομπήν; ἢ τίνες οἱ πέμποντες ἦσαν;

ΖΕΦΥΡΟΣ: Ἡδίστου θεάματος ἀπελείφθης, οἷον οὐκ ἂν ἄλλο ἴδοις ἔτι.

ἄλλος, -η, -ο: another
ἀπολείπω: to miss (+ *gen.*)
εἶδον: to see
Ζέφυρος, ὁ: Zephyrus, the west wind
ἡδύς, -εῖα, -ύ: sweet
θάλαττα, ἡ: the sea
θέαμα, -ατος, τό: a sight, show, spectacle

λέγω: to say, to mean
μεγαλοπρεπής, -ές: magnificent
Νότος, ὁ: Notos, the south wind
πέμπω: to send
πνέω: to blow
πομπή, ἡ: a procession
πώποτε: ever yet

ἀφ' οὗ: = ἀπό οὗ (sc. χρονου), "*from which time* I am" i.e. since I was born
οἱ πέμποντες: pr. part., "the ones making the procession."
ἀπελείφθης: aor. pass. of ἀπο-λείπω, "you have been left behind" + gen., i.e. you missed it
οὐκ ἂν ... ἴδοις: aor. opt. pot., "such as *you would never see* again"

ΝΟΤΟΣ: Περὶ τὴν ἐρυθρὰν γὰρ θάλατταν εἰργαζόμην, ἐπέπνευσα δὲ καὶ μέρος τῆς Ἰνδικῆς, ὅσα παράλια τῆς χώρας· οὐδὲν οὖν οἶδα ὧν λέγεις.

ΖΕΦΥΡΟΣ: Ἀλλὰ τὸν Σιδώνιόν γε Ἀγήνορα οἶδας;

ΝΟΤΟΣ: Ναί, τὸν τῆς Εὐρώπης πατέρα. τί μήν;

ΖΕΦΥΡΟΣ: Περὶ αὐτῆς ἐκείνης διηγήσομαί σοι.

ΝΟΤΟΣ: Μῶν ὅτι ὁ Ζεὺς ἐραστὴς τῆς παιδὸς ἐκ πολλοῦ; τοῦτο γὰρ καὶ πάλαι ἠπιστάμην.

ΖΕΦΥΡΟΣ: Οὐκοῦν τὸν μὲν ἔρωτα οἶσθα, τὰ μετὰ ταῦτα ἤδη ἄκουσον. ἡ μὲν Εὐρώπη κατεληλύθει ἐπὶ τὴν ἠϊόνα

Ἀγήνωρ, -ορος, ὁ: Agenor, King of Sidon
ἀκούω: to hear
διηγέομαι: to set out in detail, describe in full
ἐπιπνέω: to breathe upon, to blow freshly upon
ἐπίσταμαι: to know
ἐραστής, -οῦ, ὁ: a lover
ἐργάζομαι: to work, labour
ἐρυθρός, -ά, -όν: red
Εὐρώπη, ἡ: Europa
ἠϊών, ἠϊόνος, ἡ: a shoreline, beach
θάλαττα, ἡ: the sea
Ἰνδικός, -ή, -όν: Indian

κατέρχομαι: to go down from
λέγω: to speak
μέρος, -εος, τό: a part, share
μῶν: surely not...? *expecting a negative answer*
οἶδα: to know
οὐκοῦν: therefore, then, accordingly
παῖς, παιδός, ὁ: a child
πάλαι: long ago, for a long time
παράλιος, -α, -ον: by the sea
πατήρ, πατρός, ὁ: a father
Σιδώνιος, -α, -ον: Sidonian
χώρα, ἡ: a space, place

τὴν ἐρυθρὰν θάλατταν: the Red Sea, i.e. the Indian Ocean, indicating a distant area
ἐπέπνευσα: aor., "I blew upon"
τῆς Ἰνδικῆς ... τῆς χώρας: gen., "part *of the Indian land*"
ὅσα παράλια: "whatever was along the coast"
ὧν λέγεις: relative attracted into gen. case, "I do not know *of the things which you speak.*"
τί μήν: "what about it?"
ἐκ πολλοῦ (sc. χρονου): "from a long time"
ἠπιστάμην: impf. of ἐπίσταμαι, "I knew"
τὰ μετὰ ταῦτα: "the things after"
ἄκουσον: aor. imper., "listen!"
κατεληλύθει: plupf. of κατα-έρχομαι, "she had gone down"

παίζουσα τὰς ἡλικιώτιδας παραλαβοῦσα, ὁ Ζεὺς δὲ ταύρῳ εἰκάσας ἑαυτὸν συνέπαιζεν αὐταῖς κάλλιστος φαινόμενος: λευκός τε γὰρ ἦν ἀκριβῶς καὶ τὰ κέρατα εὐκαμπὴς καὶ τὸ βλέμμα ἥμερος: ἐσκίρτα οὖν καὶ αὐτὸς ἐπὶ τῆς ἠϊόνος καὶ ἐμυκᾶτο ἥδιστον, ὥστε τὴν Εὐρώπην τολμῆσαι καὶ ἀναβῆναι αὐτόν. ὡς δὲ τοῦτο ἐγένετο, δρομαῖος μὲν ὁ Ζεὺς ὥρμησεν ἐπὶ τὴν θάλατταν φέρων αὐτὴν καὶ ἐνήχετο ἐμπεσών, ἡ δὲ πάνυ ἐκπλαγὴς τῷ πράγματι τῇ λαιᾷ μὲν εἴχετο τοῦ κέρατος,

---

ἀκριβῶς: exactly, completely
ἀναβαίνω: to go up, mount
βλέμμα, -ατος, τό: an eye
δρομαῖος, -α, -ον: running at full speed
εἰκάζω: to make like to (+ *dat.*)
ἐκπλαγής, -ές: panic-stricken
ἐμπίπτω: to fall upon
εὐκαμπής, -ές: well-curved, curved
ἡδύς, -εῖα, -ύ: sweet
ἡλικιῶτις, -ώτιδος, ἡ: a companion
ἥμερος, -η, -ον: tamed, gentle
θάλαττα, ἡ: the sea
κάλλιστος, -η, -ον: very beautiful
κέρας, -ατος, τό: a horn

λαιός, -ά, -όν: on the left
λευκός, -ή, -όν: light, bright, brilliant
μυκάομαι: to moo
νήχομαι: to swim
ὁρμάω: to set in motion
παίζω: to play
παραλαμβάνω: to take along
σκιρτάω: to spring, leap, bound
συμπαίζω: to play or sport with
ταῦρος, ὁ: a bull
τολμάω: to dare
φαίνομαι: to appear
φέρω: to bear

παραλαβοῦσα: aor. part., "having taken along"
εἰκάσας: aor. part., "having likened himself" + dat.
συνέπαιζεν: impf., "he was playing with" + dat.
φαινόμενος: pr. part., "appearing"
τὰ κέρατα: acc. of respect, "well-curved *in respect to the horns*"
τὸ βλέμμα: acc. of respect, "gentle *in respect to the eyes*"
ἐσκίρτα: impf., "he was leaping around"
ἐμυκᾶτο: impf., "he was mooing"
ὥστε ... τολμῆσαι: aor. inf. in res. cl., "so that she dared" + inf.
ἀναβῆναι: aor. inf. supplementing τολμῆσαι, "to climb upon"
ὥρμησεν: aor., "he set off"
ἐνήχετο: impf., "he began swimming"
ἐμπεσών: aor. part., "having fallen into (the sea)"
ἡ δὲ: "but she" i.e. Europa
τῇ λαιᾷ μὲν ... τῇ ἑτέρᾳ δὲ: "with the left ... with the right"
εἴχετο: impf. of ἔχω, "she was holding on to" + gen.

Lucian

ὡς μὴ ἀπολισθάνοι, τῇ ἑτέρᾳ δὲ ἠνεμωμένον τὸν πέπλον ξυνεῖχεν.

ΝΟΤΟΣ: Ἡδὺ τοῦτο θέαμα εἶδες, ὦ Ζέφυρε, καὶ ἐρωτικόν, νηχόμενον τὸν Δία καὶ φέροντα τὴν ἀγαπωμένην.

ΖΕΦΥΡΟΣ: Καὶ μὴν τὰ μετὰ ταῦτα ἡδίω παρὰ πολύ, ὦ Νότε· ἥ τε γὰρ θάλαττα εὐθὺς ἀκύμων ἐγένετο καὶ τὴν γαλήνην ἐπισπασαμένη λείαν παρεῖχεν ἑαυτήν, ἡμεῖς δὲ πάντες ἡσυχίαν ἄγοντες οὐδὲν ἄλλο ἢ θεαταὶ μόνον τῶν γιγνομένων παρηκολουθοῦμεν, Ἔρωτες δὲ παραπετόμενοι μικρὸν ἐκ τῆς θαλάττης, ὡς ἐνίοτε

ἀγαπάω: to treat with affection, love
ἄγω: to lead, do
ἄκυμος, -ον: tranquil
ἀνεμόομαι: to be filled with wind
ἀπολισθάνω: to slip off or away
γαλήνη, ἡ: a stillness of the sea, calm
ἐνίοτε: sometimes
ἐπισπάω: to draw or drag after
Ἔρως, -ωτος, ὁ: a Love (personified), a Cupid
ἐρωτικός, -ή, -όν: amatory
ἡσυχία, ἡ: a stillness, rest, quiet

θάλαττα, ἡ: the sea
θέαμα, -ατος, τό: a sight, show, spectacle
θεατής, -ου, ὁ: a spectator
λεῖος, -α, -ον: smooth, plain
μικρός, -ά, -όν: small, little
ξυνέχω: to hold together
παρακολουθέω: to follow beside, follow closely
παραπέτομαι: to fly alongside
παρέχω: to furnish, provide, supply
πέπλος, ὁ: a woven cloth
φέρω: to bear

ὡς μὴ ἀπολισθάνοι: pr. opt. in neg. purpose clause, "lest she slip off"
ἠνεμωμένον: perf. part., "her veil *having been filled with wind*"
ξυνεῖχεν: impf. of ξυν-ἔχω, "she was holding together"
νηχόμενον ... φέροντα: pr. part. in apposition to θέαμα, "namely, Zeus swimming ... carrying"
τὴν ἀγαπωμένην: pr. part. pass., "his beloved one"
καὶ μὴν: "and yet"
ἡδίω: = (ἡδίο(ν)α), n. pl., "sweeter"
ἐπισπασαμένη: aor. part., "having drawn after"
λείαν: acc. pred., "made herself *smooth*"
παρεῖχεν: impf., "the sea *made* herself"
ἡσυχίαν ἄγοντες: "leading quiet," i.e. being quiet
οὐδὲν ἄλλο ἢ ... μόνον: acc. of respect, "as nothing other than ... only"
παραπετόμενοι: pr. part., "flying along side" + gen.
μικρὸν: acc. of extent, "*just a little bit* above the sea"

Dialogues of the Sea Gods

ἄκροις τοῖς ποσὶν ἐπιψαύειν τοῦ ὕδατος, ἡμμένας τὰς δᾷδας φέροντες ᾖδον ἅμα τὸν ὑμέναιον, αἱ Νηρηΐδες δὲ ἀναδῦσαι παρίππευον ἐπὶ τῶν δελφίνων ἐπικροτοῦσαι ἡμίγυμνοι αἱ πολλαί, τό τε τῶν Τριτώνων γένος καὶ εἴ τι ἄλλο μὴ φοβερὸν ἰδεῖν τῶν θαλαττίων ἅπαντα περιεχόρευε τὴν παῖδα: ὁ μὲν γὰρ Ποσειδῶν ἐπιβεβηκὼς ἅρματος, παροχουμένην τὴν Ἀμφιτρίτην ἔχων, προῆγε γεγηθὼς ὁδοποιῶν νηχομένῳ τῷ ἀδελφῷ: ἐπὶ πᾶσι δὲ

ἀδελφός, ὁ: a brother
ᾄδω: to sing
ἄκρος, -α, -ον: at the furthest point
ἅμα: at the same time
Ἀμφιτρίτη, ἡ: Amphitrite, wife of Poseidon
ἀναδύω: to come to the top of water
ἅπας, ἅπασα, ἅπαν: all, every, whole
ἅπτω: to touch, kindle (fire)
ἅρμα, -ατος, τό: a chariot
γένος, -ους, τό: a race, stock, family
γηθέω: to rejoice
δαΐς, δαΐδος, ἡ: a torch
δελφίς, -ῖνος, ὁ: a dolphin
ἐπιβαίνω: to go upon, mount
ἐπικροτέω: to rattle over
ἐπιψαύω: to touch lightly

ἡμίγυμνος, -ον: half-naked
θαλάττιος, -α, -ον: belonging to the sea
Νηρεΐδες, αἱ: the Nereids
νήχομαι: to swim
ὁδοποιέω: to make a path for
παριππεύω: to ride along or over
παροχέομαι: to sit beside in a chariot
περιχορεύω: to dance around
Ποσειδῶν, -ῶνος, ὁ: Poseidon
πούς, -δος, ὁ: a foot
προάγω: to lead forward, on, onward
Τρίτων, -ωνος, ὁ: Triton
ὕδωρ, ὕδατος, τό: water
ὑμέναιος, ὁ: a wedding or bridal song
φέρω: to bear
φοβερός, -ά, -όν: fearful

ὡς ... ἐπιψαύειν: pr. inf. in result clause, "*so that they touch* the water"
ἄκροις τοῖς ποσὶν: dat. of means, "with the tips of their feet"
ἡμμένας: perf. part., "torches *having been lit*"
ᾖδον: impf., "they were singing"
ἀναδῦσαι: aor. part., "having come to the surface"
παρίππευον: impf. of **παρα-ιππεύω**, "they were riding along"
ἐπικροτοῦσαι: pr. part., "making rattling sounds"
εἴ τι ἄλλο: "and any other"
ἰδεῖν: aor. inf. epex. after **φοβερὸν**, "not frightening *to see*"
ἐπιβεβηκὼς: perf. part., "having mounted" + gen.
παροχουμένην: pr. part., "Amphitrite *sitting beside*"
γεγηθὼς: perf. part., "delighted"
ὁδοποιῶν: pr. part., "making a path"
ἀδελφῷ: dat. of advant., "for his brother"
ἐπὶ πᾶσι δὲ: "but in addition to everything else"

Lucian

τὴν Ἀφροδίτην δύο Τρίτωνες ἔφερον ἐπὶ κόγχης κατακειμένην, ἄνθη παντοῖα ἐπιπάττουσαν τῇ νύμφῃ. ταῦτα ἐκ Φοινίκης ἄχρι τῆς Κρήτης ἐγένετο· ἐπεὶ δὲ ἐπέβη τῇ νήσῳ ὁ μὲν ταῦρος οὐκέτι ἐφαίνετο, ἐπιλαβόμενος δὲ τῆς χειρὸς ὁ Ζεὺς ἀπῆγε τὴν Εὐρώπην εἰς τὸ Δικταῖον ἄντρον ἐρυθριῶσαν καὶ κάτω ὁρῶσαν· ἠπίστατο γὰρ ἤδη ἐφ᾽ ὅτῳ ἄγοιτο. ἡμεῖς δὲ ἐμπεσόντες ἄλλο ἄλλος τοῦ πελάγους μέρος διεκυμαίνομεν.

ΝΟΤΟΣ: Ὦ μακάριε Ζέφυρε τῆς θέας· ἐγὼ δὲ γρῦπας καὶ ἐλέφαντας καὶ μέλανας ἀνθρώπους ἑώρων.

ἄγω: to lead
ἄνθος, τό: a blossom, flower
ἄντρον, τό: a cave
ἀπάγω: to lead away, carry off
Ἀφροδίτη, ἡ: Aphrodite
ἄχρι: all the way to (+ *gen.*)
γρύψ, -πος, ὁ: a griffin
διακυμαίνω: to raise into waves
Δικταῖος, -η, -ον: of Mount Dicté
ἐλέφας, -αντος, ὁ: an elephant
ἐμπίπτω: to fall upon
ἐπιβαίνω: to go upon
ἐπιλαμβάνω: to take hold of (+ *gen.*)
ἐπιπάττω: to sprinkle
ἐπίσταμαι: to know
ἐρυθριάω: to blush
θέα, ἡ: a seeing, looking at

κατάκειμαι: to lie down, lie outstretched
κάτω: down, downwards
κόγχη, ἡ: a mussel or cockle
Κρήτη, ἡ: Crete
μακάριος: blessed, happy
μέλας, μέλαινα, μέλαν: black
μέρος, -εος, τό: a part, share
νῆσος, ἡ: an island
νύμφη, ἡ: a young wife, bride
οὐκέτι: no more, no longer, no further
παντοῖος, -α, -ον: of all sorts or kinds, manifold
πέλαγος, -ους, τό: the sea
ταῦρος, ὁ: a bull
φαίνομαι: to appear
Φοινίκη, ἡ: Phoenicia
χείρ, χειρός, ἡ: a hand

κατακειμένην ... ἐπιπάττουσαν: pr. part., "Aphrodite *lying down ... sprinkling*"
ἐπέβη: aor., "when *he went upon*" + dat.
ἐπιλαβόμενος: aor. part., "having taken hold of" + gen.
ἐρυθριῶσαν: pr. part. acc., "her *blushing*"
ἠπίστατο: impf., "she knew"
ἐφ᾽ ὅτῳ ἄγοιτο: pr. opt. pass. in ind. quest. after **ἠπίστατο**, "she knew *on account of what she was being led*"
ἐμπεσόντες: aor. part., "we *having fallen upon*"
ἄλλο ... μέρος: "*a different part* of the sea"
ἄλλος: in apposition to **ἡμεῖς**, "a different one (of us)"
τῆς θέας: gen. exclam., "what a sight!"
ἑώρων: impf. of **ὁράω**, "I was seeing"

List of Verbs

List of Verbs

The following is a list of verbs that have some irregularity in their conjugation. Contract verbs and other verbs that are completely predictable (-ίζω, -εύω, etc.) are generally not included. The principal parts of the Greek verb in order are 1. Present 2. Future 3. Aorist 4. Perfect Active 5. Perfect Middle 6. Aorist Passive, 7. Future Passive. We have not included the future passive below, since it is very rare. For many verbs not all forms are attested or are only poetic. Verbs are alphabetized under their main stem, followed by various compounds that occur in the *Dialogues of the Sea Gods*, with a brief definition. A dash (-) before a form means that it occurs only or chiefly with a prefix. The list is based on the list of verbs in H. Smyth, *A Greek Grammar*.

ἄγω: to lead ἄξω, 2 aor. ἤγαγον, ἦχα, ἦγμαι, ἤχθην
    ἀπάγω: to lead away, divert
    προσάγω: to bring to or upon
    ὑπάγω: to lead or bring under

ᾄδω: to sing ᾄσομαι, ᾖσα, ᾖσμαι, ᾔσθην

αἰδέομαι: to feel shame αἰδέσομαι, ᾔδεσμαι, ᾐδέσθην

αἰσθάνομαι: to perceive αἰσθήσομαι, 2 aor. ᾐσθόμην, ᾔσθημαι

ἀκούω: to hear ἀκούσομαι, ἤκουσα, 2 perf. ἀκήκοα, 2 plup. ἠκηκόη or ἀκηκόη, ἠκούσθην

ἁλίσκομαι: to be taken ἁλώσομαι, 2 aor. ἑάλων, ἑάλωκα

ἀλλάττω: to change ἀλλάξω, ἤλλαξα, -ήλλαχα, ἤλλαγμαι, ἠλλάχθην or ἠλλάγην
    διαλλάττω: to change, become different

ἅπτω: to fasten, (mid.) to touch ἅψω, ἦψα, ἧμμαι, ἥφθην

ἀρύω: to draw (water) ἐρύσομαι, ἤρυσα -ηρύθην

ἄρχω: to be first, begin ἄρξω, ἦρξα, ἦργμαι, ἤρχθην

αἱρέω: to take αἱρήσω, 2 aor. εἷλον, ᾕρηκα, ᾕρημαι, ᾑρέθην
    ἀφαιρέω: to take away, exclude, set aside, remove

ἀφικνέομαι: to arrive at ἀφ-ίξομαι, 2 aor. ἀφ-ικόμην, ἀφ-ῖγμαι

ἄχθομαι: to be vexed ἀχθέσομαι, ἠχθέσθην

βαίνω: to step βήσομαι, 2 aor. ἔβην, βέβηκα
    ἀναβαίνω: to go up
    ἐπιβαίνω: to go upon, trample
    συμβαίνω: to come together, come to pass

βάλλω: to throw βαλῶ, 2 aor. ἔβαλον, βέβληκα, βέβλημαι, ἐβλήθην
    μεταβάλλω: to change quickly
    ἐμβάλλω: to throw in

γαμέω: to marry γαμῶ, ἔγημα, γεγάμηκα

γίνομαι: to become γενήσομαι, 2 aor. ἐγενόμην, 2 perf. γέγονα, γεγένημαι, ἐγενήθην
    παραγίνομαι: to be present, attend

γιγνώσκω: to know γνώσομαι, ἔγνων, ἔγνωκα, ἔγνωσμαι, ἐγνώσθην
    διαγινώσκω: to distinguish, discern, resolve

γράφω: to write γράψω, ἔγραψα, γέγραφα, γέγραμμαι, ἐγράφην
    ἐπιγράφω: to write upon, inscribe, dedicate

δείκνυμι: to show δείξω, ἔδειξα, δέδειχα, δέδειγμαι, ἐδείχθην
    προδείκνυμι: to display forth

δέω: to need, lack (mid.) ask: δεήσω, ἐδέησα, δεδέηκα, δεδέημαι, ἐδεήθην

δέχομαι: to receive δέξομαι, ἐδεξάμην, δέδεγμαι, -εδέχθην
    ὑποδέχομαι: to receive beneath

διδάσκω: to teach, (mid.) learn διδάξω, ἐδίδαξα, δεδίδαχα, δεδίδαγμαι, ἐδιδάχθην

δίδωμι: to give δώσω, 1 aor. ἔδωκα in s., 2 aor. ἔδομεν in pl. δέδωκα, δέδομαι, ἐδόθην
    ἀναδίδωμι: to give up
    ἀποδίδωμι: to give back, return, render

διώκω: to pursue διώξομαι, ἐδίωξα, δεδίωχα, ἐδιώχθην

δοκέω: to think, seem δόξω, ἔδοξα, δέδογμαι

δύω: to go down δύσω, -έδυσα (trans.), 2 aor. ἔδυν (intrans.), δέδυκα, -δέδυμαι, -εδύθην
    ἀναδύω: to come to the surface
    καταδύω: to go down, sink
    ὑποδύω: to plunge below

ἐγείρω: to wake up ἐγερῶ, ἤγειρα, 2 perf. ἐγρήγορα, ἐγήγερμαι, ἠγέρθην
    ἀνεγείρω: to wake up, rouse

ἐθέλω: to wish ἐθελήσω, ἠθέλησα, ἠθέληκα

εἶδον: used as aorist of ὁράω. See page 23.

εἰκάζω: to make like εἰκάσω, ἤκασα, ἤκασμαι, ἠκάσθην

εἶμι: to go; see ἔρχομαι

εἰμί: to be, fut. ἔσομαι, impf. ἦν
    πάρειμι: to be present, stand by
    πρόσειμι: to be present, possible
    σύνειμι: to be with, have intercourse with

ἐλέγχω: examine, confute: ἐλέγξω, ἤλεγξα, ἐλήλεγμαι, ἠλέγχθην.

ἐπίσταμαι: understand ἐπιστήσομαι, ἠπιστήθην.

ἐράω: to love, imp. ἤρων aor. ἠράσθην

ἐργάζομαι: to work, ἐργάσομαι, ἠργασάμην, εἴργασμαι, ἠργάσθην.

ἔρχομαι: to come or go to fut. εἶμι, 2 aor. ἦλθον, 2 perf. ἐλήλυθα
    ἀπέρχομαι: to go away, depart from
    ἐπέρχομαι: to go upon, attack
    κατέρχομαι: to go down from
    μετέρχομαι: to go among, pursue
    προσέρχομαι: to come to, approach
    ὑπεξέρχομαι: to go out secretly
    ὑπέρχομαι: to go under

ἐρωτάω: to ask, ἐρήσομαι, 2 aor. ἠρόμην

εὑρίσκω: to find εὑρήσω, 2 aor. ηὗρον or εὗρον, ηὕρηκα or εὕρηκα, εὕρημαι, εὑρέθην

εὔχομαι: to pray εὔξομαι, ηὐξάμην, ηὖγμαι

ἔχω: to have ἕξω, 2 aor. ἔσχον, ἔσχηκα, imperf. εἶχον.
    ἀντέχω: to hold against
    ἀπέχω: to keep off, hold back
    ἐπέχω: to hold back
    κατέχω: to hold fast
    παρέχω: to provide, allow
    προσέχω: to hold to
    συνέχω: to hold together
    ὑπέχω: to hold under

ζάω: to live ζήσω, ἔζησα, ἔζηκα

ζεύγνυμι: to yoke ζεύξω, ἔζευξα, ἔζευγμαι, ἐζεύχθην

ἡγέομαι: to go before, consider ἡγήσομαι, ἡγησάμην, ἥγημαι
    διηγέομαι: to set out in detail, describe in full

θάπτω: to bury θάψω, ἔθαψα, τέθαμμαι, ἐτάφην

θνῄσκω: to die θανοῦμαι, 2 aor. -έθανον, τέθνηκα
    ἀποθνῄσκω: to die

ἵημι: to let go, relax, to send forth ἥσω, ἧκα, εἷκα, εἷμαι, εἵθην
    ἀφίημι: to send forth, send away
    καθίημι: to set down
    παρίημι: to disregard, allow past
    συνίημι: to bring or set together

ἵστημι: to make to stand, set στήσω shall set, ἔστησα set, caused to stand, 2 aor. ἔστην stood, 1 perf. ἕστηκα stand, plupf. εἱστήκη stood, ἐστάθην
    διίστημι: to set apart, separate
    παρίστημι: to stand up beside
    περιίστημι: to place round
    ξυνίστημι: to set together, combine, unite

καίω: to burn καύσω, ἔκαυσα, -κέκαυκα, κέκαυμαι, ἐκαύθην
    ἀνακαίω: to light up

καλέω: to call καλῶ, ἐκάλεσα, κέκληκα, κέκλημαι, ἐκλήθην
    συγκαλέω: to call to council, convoke, convene

κεῖμαι: to lie, be placed: κείσομαι.

κρίνω: to decide κρινῶ, ἔκρινα, κέκρικα, κέκριμαι, ἐκρίθην

κρύπτω to hide from κρύψω, ἔκρυψα, κέκρυμμαι, ἐκρύφθην
    συνκρύπτω: to hide together
    ἀποκρύπτω: to hide from, keep hidden from

κτείνω: to kill κτενῶ, ἔκτεινα, 2 perf. –έκτονα
    ἀποκτείνω: to kill, slay

λαμβάνω: to take λήψομαι, ἔλαβον, εἴληφα, εἴλημμαι, ἐλήφθην
    ἀναλαμβάνω: to take up, take into one's hands
    ἐπιλαμβάνω: to lay hold of, seize, attack
    καταλαμβάνω: to seize, overtake
    παραλαμβάνω: to take beside
    συλλαμβάνω: to collect, seize
    ὑπολαμβάνω: to undertake, to understand

λανθάνω: to escape notice λήσω, ἔλαθον, λέληθα

λέγω: to speak ἐρέω, εἶπον, εἴρηκα, λέλεγμαι, ἐλέχθην and ἐρρήθην

λείπω: to leave λείψω, ἔλιπον, λέλοιπα, λέλειμμαι, ἐλείφθην
    ἀπολείπω: to leave behind

μανθάνω: to learn μαθήσομαι, ἔμαθον, μεμάθηκα

μεθύσκω: to make drunk ἐμέθυσα, ἐμεθύσθην

μέμφομαι: to blame μέμψομαι, ἐμεμψάμην, ἐμέμφθην

μένω: to stay μενῶ, ἔμεινα, μεμένηκα

μίγνυμι: to mix μείξω, ἔμειξα, μέμειγμαι, ἐμείχθην

οἶδα: to know, perf. of εἶδον. See page 23.

οἴγνυμι: to open, -οίξω, -έῳξα, -έῳχα, -έῳγμαι, -εῴχθην
    ἀνοίγνυμι: to open up

ὄλλυμι: to destroy ὀλῶ, -ώλεσα, -ολώλεκα, -όλωλα
    ἀπόλλυμι: to destroy, lose

ὁράω: to see, ὄψομαι, 2 aor. εἶδον, ἑόρακα and ἑώρακα, ὤφθην, imperf. ἑώρων
    ὑπεροράω: to look down upon, overlook

πάσχω: to experience πείσομαι, 2 aor. ἔπαθον, 2 perf. πέπονθα

πέμπω: to convey πέμψω, ἔπεμψα, 2 perf. πέπομφα, πέπεμμαι, ἐπέμφθην
    ἐκπέμπω: to send out or forth from
    ἐπιπέμπω: to send against
    μεταπέμπω: to send after, send for, summon
    παραπέμπω: to convey, escort

πέτομαι: to fly πτήσομαι, –επτάμην, πεπότημαι, ἐπετάσθην
    ἀναπέτομαι: to fly up
    παραπέτομαι: to fly alongside

πήγνυμι: to form together, congeal πήξω, ἔπηξα, 2 perf. πέπηγα, 2 aor. pass. ἐπάγην

πίνω: to drink πίομαι, 2 aor. ἔπιον, πέπωκα, -πέπομαι, -επόθην
    καταπίνω: to gulp, swallow down

πίπτω: to fall πεσοῦμαι, 2 aor. ἔπεσον, πέπτωκα
    καταπίπτω: to fall or drop down

πλέω: to sail πλεύσομαι, ἔπλευσα, πέπλευκα, πέπλευσμαι, ἐπλεύσθην
    ἀναπλέω: to sail upstream

πνέω: to blow πνεύσομαι, ἔπνευσα, -πέπνευκα
    ἐπιπνέω: to blow upon

πράττω: to do πράξω, ἔπραξα, 2 perf. πέπραχα, πέπραγμαι, ἐπράχθην

πυνθάνομαι: to learn πεύσομαι, 2 aor. ἐπυθόμην, πέπυσμαι

ῥέω: to flow ῥυήσομαι, ἐρρύην, ἐρρύηκα

σκώπτω: to mock σκώψομαι, ἔσκωψα, ἐσκώφθην

σπάω: to draw σπάσω, ἔσπασα, -έσπακα, ἔσπασμαι, -εσπάσθην
    ἀνασπάω: to draw up
    ἀποσπάω: to tear away
    ἐπισπάω: to draw or drag after
    κατσπάω: to drag down

στέλλω: to send, arrange στελῶ, ἔστειλα, -έσταλκα, ἔσταλμαι, 2 aor. pass. ἐστάλην

στρέφω: to turn στρέψω, ἔστρεψα, ἔστραμμαι, ἐστρέφθην
    ἀναστρέφω: to turn back, return

σῴζω: to save σώσω, ἔσωσα, σέσωκα, ἐσώθην

τίθημι: to place θήσω, ἔθηκα, τέθηκα, τέθειμαι (but usu. κεῖμαι), ἐτέθην
    ἀνατίθημι: to put up
    ἐπιτίθημι: to put upon, add to

τίκτω: to beget, bring forth: τέξομαι, 2 aor. ἔτεκον, 2 perf. τέτοκα, ἐτέχθην

τέμνω: to cut τεμῶ, 2 aor. ἔτεμον, -τέτμηκα, τέτμημαι, ἐτμήθην
    ἀποτέμνω: to cut off, sever

τρέπω: to turn τρέψω, ἔτρεψα, 2 aor. mid. ἐτράπομην, τέτραμμαι, ἐτράμην
    ἐπιτρέπω: to turn towards, agree

τυγχάνω: to happen τεύξομαι, ἔτυχον, τετύχηκα. τέτυγμαι, ἐτύχθην
    ἐντυγχάνω: to fall in with, meet with

φαίνω: to show, (mid.) appear φανῶ, ἔφηνα, πέφηνα, πέφασμαι, ἐφάνην
    προφαίνω: to bring forth, bring to light

φέρω: to bear οἴσω, 1 aor. ἤνεγκα, 2 aor. ἤνεγκον, 2 perf. ἐνήνοχα, perf. mid. ἐνήνεγμαι, ἠνέχθην
    καταφέρω: to bring down
    περιφέρω: to carry around
    προσφέρω: to bring to or upon, approach

φεύγω: to flee φεύξομαι, ἔφυγον, πέφευγα
    διαφεύγω: to flee, get away, escape

φράζω: to point out, tell φράσω, ἔφρασα, πέφρακα, πέφρασμαι, ἐφράσθην

φυλάττω: to guard φυλάξω, ἐφύλαξα, πεφύλαχα, πεφύλαγμαι, ἐφυλάχθην

χαίρω: to rejoice at χαιρήσω, κεχάρηκα, κεχάρημαι, ἐχάρην

Glossary

Glossary

A α

ἄγριος, -α, -ον: cruel, savage
ἀλλά: otherwise, but
ἄλλος, -η, -ον: another, other
ἄγω: to lead or carry, to convey, bring
ἀδελφή, ἡ: a sister
ἀδελφός, ὁ: a brother
ἀδικέω: to do wrong, harm
ᾄδω: to sing
ἀεί: always
ἀθλίος, -α, -ον: miserable
ἀκούω: to hear
ἀκριβῶς: accurately, exactly
ἅμα: at the same time, together with (+ *dat.*)
ἀμείνων, -ον: better
ἄμορφος, -ον: misshapen, unsightly
ἄν: (*indefinite particle; generalizes dependent clauses with subjunctive; indicates contrary-to-fact with independent clauses in the indicative; potentiality with the optative*)
ἀναδύνω: to come to the top of water
ἀναλαμβάνω: to take up, take into one's hands
ἀναφαίνω: to show, make visible
ἀνήρ, ἀνδρός ὁ: a man
ἄνθρωπος, ὁ: a man
ἀξιόω: to think worthy
ἀντί: instead of (+ *gen.*)
ἅπας, ἅπασα, ἅπαν: all, every, whole
ἀπέρχομαι: to go away
ἀπιστέω: to disbelieve
ἀπό: from, away from (+ *gen.*)
ἀποθνήσκω: to die
ἀπόλλυμι: to destroy utterly, kill, slay
ἅρμα, -ατος, τό: a chariot
αὖθις: back, again
αὐτός, -ή, -ό: he, she, it; self, same
ἄχρι: up to (+ *gen.*)

B β

βρέφος, -εος, τό: a newborn

Γ γ

γαλήνη, ἡ: a stillness of the sea, calm
γάμος, τό: a wedding, marriage
γάρ: for
γε: at least, at any rate (postpositive)
γένος, -ους, τό: a race, stock, family
γῆ, ἡ: earth, shore
γίγνομαι: to become, happen, occur
γοῦν: at any rate, any way
γυνή, γυναικός, ἡ: a woman

Δ δ

δακρύω: to weep, shed tears
δέ: and, but, on the other hand (preceded by *μέν*)
δεῖ: it is necessary
δείκνυμι: to bring to light, display, exhibit
δεινός, -ή, -όν: fearful, terrible
δελφίς, -ῖνος, ὁ: a dolphin
δῆλος, -ον: visible, conspicuous
διά: through (+ *gen.*); with, by means of (+ *acc.*)
δίδωμι: to give
δοκέω: to seem
δύναμαι: to be able
δύο: two

Ε ε

ἐγώ, μου: I, my
ἐθέλω: to will, wish, purpose

Glossary

εἰ: if
εἶδον: to see (*aor.*)
εἰμί: to be
εἶπον: to say (*aor.*)
εἰς, ἐς: into, to (+ *acc.*)
εἶτα: next, then
εἴτε... εἴτε: whether... or
ἐκ, ἐξ: from, out of, after (+ *gen.*)
ἐκεῖνος, -η, -ον: that, that one
ἐλεέω: to have pity on, show mercy upon
ἐμαυτοῦ: of me, of myself
ἐμβάλλω: to throw in, put in
ἐμπίπτω: to fall upon
ἐν: in, at, among (+ *dat.*)
ἔνθα: where, there
ἐνταῦθα: here, there
ἔοικα: to seem, to be likely (+ *inf.*)
ἐπαινέω: to approve, applaud, commend
ἐπεί: since
ἐπειδάν: whenever (+ *subj.*)
ἐπέραστος, -ον: lovely, amiable
ἐπί: at (+ *gen.*); on, upon (+ *dat.*); on to, against (+ *acc.*)
ἐπιβαίνω: to go upon, mount
ἐπιβουλεύω: to plan or contrive against
ἐπιπρέπω: to be visible in addition to (+ *dat.*)
ἐπίσταμαι: to know
ἐραστής, -οῦ, ὁ: a lover
ἐράω: to love
ἐργάζομαι: to work, affect, make
ἔρως, -ωτος, ὁ: love
ἐρωτικός, -ή, -όν: amatory
ἔτι: still
εὖ: well
εὐθύς: straightaway, directly
ἔχω: to have, hold; to be able (+ *inf.*)

Z ζ

H η

ἤ: or; than
ἤδη: already, now
ἡδύς, -εῖα, -ύ: sweet
ἥκω: to have come, be present

Θ θ

θάλαττα, ἡ: the sea
θάπτω: to bury
θεός, ὁ: a god
θνῄσκω: to die
θυγάτηρ, -έρος, ἡ: a daughter
θύρα, ἡ: a door

I ι

ἱκανός, -η, -ον: becoming, befitting, sufficing
ἵστημι: to make to stand
ἰχθύς, ὁ: a fish

K κ

καθίζω: to make to sit down, seat
καί: and, also, even
καίτοι: and yet
κάκος, -α, -ον: trouble, evil
κακός, -ή, -όν: bad
καλέω: to call
καλλίων, κάλλιον: more beautiful
καλός, -η, -ον: beautiful
κατά, καθ': down, along, according to (+ *acc.*)
κέρας, -ατος, τό: a horn
κῆτος, -εος, τό: a sea monster

κιβωτός, ἡ: a wooden box, chest, coffer
κομίζω: to take care of, to convey to
κόρη, ἡ: a maiden
κριός, ὁ: a ram

Λ λ

λαμβάνω: to take
λανθάνω: to escape notice
λάσιος, -ον: hairy, rough, shaggy, woolly
λέγω: to speak, say
λευκός, -ή, -όν: light, white, brilliant

Μ μ

μάλα: very
μανθάνω: to learn
μέν: on the one hand (followed by δέ)
μέσος, -η, -ον: middle, in the middle
μετά: with (+ *gen.*); after (+ *acc.*)
μεταβάλλω: to change, alter
μεταξύ: between (+ *gen.*)
μή: not; lest; don't (+ *aor. subj.* or *imper.*)
μηκέτι: no more, no longer
μήτηρ, μητρός, ἡ: a mother
μικρός, -ά, -όν: small, little
μόνος, -η, -ον: alone, only

Ν ν

ναί: yes
ναύτης, -ου, ὁ: a sailor
νεανίας, -ου, ὁ: a young man, youth
νεκρός, ὁ: a dead body, corpse
νῆσος, ἡ: an island
νήχομαι: to swim
νῦν, νυνί: now, at this moment

Ξ ξ

Ο ο

ὁ, ἡ, τό: the (*definite article*); who, which (*relative pronoun*)
ὁδός, ἡ: a way, path, track, road
οἶδα: to know
οἶμαι: to suppose, think, deem
ὅλος, -η, -ον: whole, entire
ὅμως: nevertheless
ὁπότε: when, whenever
ὅπως: as, in such manner as, how
ὁράω: to see
ὅσος, -η, -ον: what sort of
ὅσπερ: the very one, the very thing
ὅτι: that, because
οὐ, οὐκ: not
οὐδέ: but not
οὐκέτι: no more, no longer
οὐκοῦν: therefore, then, accordingly
οὖν: so, therefore
οὔτε: and not
οὔτις, οὔτι: no one, nothing
οὗτος, αὕτη, τοῦτο: this
ὀφθαλμός, ὁ: an eye

Π π

πάγκαλος, -η, -ον: all beautiful, good or noble
παῖς, παιδός, ὁ: a child
πάνυ: altogether, entirely, very
παρά: from (+ *gen.*); beside (+ *dat.*); to (+ *acc.*)
παράδοξος, -ον: paradoxical
πάρειμι: to be present
παρέχω: to furnish, provide, supply
παρθένος, ἡ: a maid
πᾶς, πᾶσα, πᾶν: all, every, whole
πάσχω: to suffer, experience
πατήρ, πατρός, ὁ: a father
πέλαγος, -ους, τό: the sea
πέμπω: to send

Glossary

περί: concerning, about (+ *gen.*); about, around (+ *acc.*)
πέτρα, ἡ: a rock, a ledge or shelf of rock
πηγή, ἡ: running waters, streams
πίνω: to drink
πλέω: to sail, go by sea
πλησίον: nearby, next to (+ *gen.*)
ποιέω: to make, to do
ποιμήν, -ένος, ὁ: a herdsman
πολύς, πολλή, πολύ: many, much
ποῦ, που: where? somewhere
πρᾶγμα, -ατος, τό: a deed, act, matter
πράττω: to do
πρό: before
πρός: to, near (+ *dat.*), from (+ *gen.*), towards (+ *acc.*)
πῦρ, τό: fire
πῶς: how? in what way?

Ρ ρ

Σ σ ς

σύ: you
σῴζω: to save

Τ τ

τε: and (*postpositive*)
τέκνον, τό: a child
τίκτω: to give birth
τις, τι: someone, something (*indefinite*)
τίς, τί: who? which? (*interrogative*)
τυγχανω: to happen to (+ *part.*)

Υ υ

ὕδωρ, ὕδατος, τό: water
υἱός, ὁ: a son
ὑπέρ: over, above (+ *gen.*); over, beyond (+ *acc.*)

ὑπό: from under, by (+ *gen.*); under (+ *dat.*); toward (+ *acc.*)
ὑποδέχομαι: to receive beneath

Φ φ

φαίνομαι: to appear, to seem
φέρω: to bear, to bring
φημί: to say, declare, make known
φοβέω: to frighten
φυλάττω: to guard, keep safe

Χ χ

χαίρω: to rejoice, be glad, be delighted
χείρ, χειρός, ἡ: a hand
χρή: it is necessary
χρυσός, ὁ: gold

Ψ ψ

Ω ω

ὡς: *adv.* as, so, how; *conj.* that, in order that, since; *prep.* to (+ *acc.*); as if, as (+ *part.*); as ____ as possible (+ *superlative*)
ὥσπερ: just as
ὥστε: with the result that, and so

NOTES

NOTES

NOTES

NOTES

NOTES

NOTES

NOTES

NOTES

NOTES

NOTES

www.ingramcontent.com/pod-product-compliance
Lightning Source LLC
Chambersburg PA
CBHW070647050426
42451CB00008B/301